Hot Wheels VW Bus Price Guide

1996-2015

2015 Edition, Volume I
(Includes Mattel & Liberty Promotions Models)

© 2015 NCHWA Publications, Apex, North Carolina. All rights reserved. No portion of this publication may be reproduced or transmitted in any form or by any means, electronic or mechanical, including photocopy, recording, or any information storage and retrieval system, without permission in writing from NCHWA.com, except by a reviewer who may quote brief passages in a critical article or review to be printed in a magazine or newspaper, or electronically transmitted on radio, television or the Internet.

HOT WHEELS and associated trademarks and trade dress are owned by Mattel, Inc.

© 2015 Mattel, Inc. All Rights Reserved. Mattel makes no representation as to the authenticity of the materials contained herein. All opinions are those of the author, and not of Mattel. This publication is derived from the author's independent research.

The NCHWA "Phoenix" is © 2015 and owned by NCHWA.com

All Hot Wheels images and art are owned by Mattel, Inc. © 2015 Mattel, Inc. All Rights Reserved.

Cover photography credit: Cherie Giordano
Interior Cover Photography Credit: Jim Martin

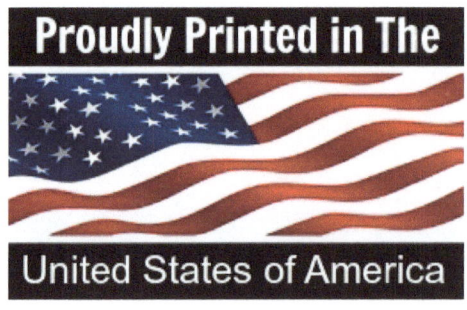

Table of Contents

Acknowledgments	1
Forward	2
About This Guide	4
Mattel Bus Values	5
Liberty Promotions Bus Values	30
Charity/Misc. LP Issues	56
Liberty Rebel Run Gallery	64
Interview With Lee Pearlman	80
Pope Designs Gallery	83
Interview With Bryan Pope	88
Production Charts	89
Top 25 Mattel Buses	90
Top 25 Liberty Promotions Buses	91
VW Bus Wheel Chart	92
Accessories	93
VW Bus Posters/Artwork	94
About The Author	98
Mattel Buses Index	100
Liberty Buses Index	102
Photo Credits	104
Other Titles by Neal Giordano	105

Acknowledgements

I never guessed I'd be putting out another publication related to Hot Wheels after completing the "Treasure Hunt Price Guide." But, here it is.

I've always said that extreme familiarity with something you really like allows you to become pretty knowledgeable over the years. I actually DO collect the VW Bus casting, and have a countless number of them on the wall in the Hot Wheels room. This model caught my eye back in 1996, when it was first issued…and it's been one of my most-collected Hot Wheels castings since then. I've been tracking them on the website since 1998 or so, and it's been a quite a project in keeping up with all of the releases over the years.

There are many incarnations of the Bus, from Mattel Issues, Liberty Promotions, Convention, Retail and Code 3's. This guide in particular will focus on the Mattel-issued and Liberty Promotions buses.

With all of that being said, one can always write a book, but there are so many driving forces behind the writer. For me, those are the following:

Mom & Dad, for buying me all those Hot Wheels back in the late 70's, crazy 80's. **Elliot Handler, Mattel Founder:** For sticking to his guns, being right and taking on the mighty Matchbox! RIP.
Phil Riehlman, for knowing he had a winner with the Bus, and pushing for its completion despite several setbacks. **Larry Wood & All past/present Hot Wheels Designers,** for fueling childhood adventures and imaginations! **The K*Mart 7:** Members who started the NCHWA as a club with me on that frigid day in February, 1998. My Kids, **Carson, Cherie and Anthony** for growing up in this hobby…pretty much with me! ;) **Joe and Vinny Garceau**, my buddies in crime, growing up; I'm still laughing my butt off. **Jennifer Walter**, despite all of the eye-rolling and general disdain for Hot Wheels…for still loving me! **Justin Edwards & Family**: I couldn't ask for a better best friend or "adopted family!" **All Former NCHWA Club Members**, from back in the day.

I also have to give major props to **Lee Pearlman**, Creative Director of Liberty Promotions. Lee was absolutely instrumental in speaking with me, even when he was swamped. He also provided me with an outstanding plethora of information and pictures in regard to the Liberty Promotions line of VW Buses. Lee is amazingly passionate about his company's work, and I'm stoked to include the Liberty buses in this book!

A book of this nature can be difficult to put together without some assistance, and my gratitude goes out to **Cherie Giordano, Jim Martin** (JWM3 on HWC.com) and **Brad Bannach** (BigBadBrad01 on HWC.com). Their outstanding photography really helped make the VW Bus Guide shine! THANK YOU, THANK YOU, THANK YOU!

Last, but not least…a huge shout-out to all of the collectors and website supporters who have emailed me with feedback, questions and suggestions. Your input is not only vital…but appreciated. Thank you, all.

~Neal Giordano

I often wonder if Phil Riehlman, the designer of the VW Bus casting, had any true idea of the waves that would be made when his creation was released! I can remember the day I was introduced to the VW Bus very clearly: Summertime, 1996. I was standing in front of the diecast aisle in Wal*Mart, when I noticed a very cool, blue Volkswagen Bus. As soon as I held it in my hand, I knew it was something special and more than just #6 of 12 in the 1996 First Editions Series. I noticed the weight; this model weighed 4 or 5 times more than regular Hot Wheels, it seemed. Cool blue paint. Vibrant red and yellow logo on the side. I was impressed. Irrelevant in the end; I needed it to add to my 1996 FE Series, so I threw it in the cart.

Fast forward, two weeks later. Word on the streets and at the diecast dealers is that the VW Bus is HOT! It immediately begins selling for $10.00 on the secondary markets, and becomes very difficult to find. It hits values anywhere from $25.00+ and peaks at around $100.00 before it becomes impossible to find. Everyone's looking for the Bus! Needless to say, I never saw another one on the pegs, or at retail for that matter.

Little did anyone know at that time that the VW Bus would become a major catalyst in re-igniting the Hot Wheels hobby. Yes, the 1995 New Model Series was a hit, and the "series concept" of numbering the cars and providing a ton of obvious variations certainly drew collectors back in. The new concept of the Treasure Hunt also added a nice twist. But, the hobby was still lacking a workhorse of sorts; something to really put Hot Wheels back onto the map. In comes the 1996 collecting year. Changes are in the wind. The New Model Series is changed to the First Editions Series, and we're introduced to the VW Bus. No one knew it was coming. As a matter of fact, the printing on the reverse of the cards stated that #6 in the 1996 FE Series was something called "Rocket Shot." The FE that never was.

Of course, the Bus wasn't issued in the same quantities as the regular First Editions. It's never been substantiated, but the general consensus is that a quantity of roughly 100,000 buses were issued into the line.

Rumors abound concerning the "real deal" with the Bus, as to why it was a short run. You'd hear that it was "too heavy, and it was a problem shipping," or "it was breaking out of the blister packs during shipping." Needless to say, these scenarios were NOT the case. The main reason for the short run was the cost; the Bus was, for obvious reasons, more expensive to produce than the other standard First Edition castings.

Origins: In an interview with Phil Riehlman, he stated that the casting was originally designed to be a "billboard" or "premium" vehicle to utilize when doing promotions for other companies, and it was simply introduced into the Mainline at a smaller run number than the other 11 cars. It was Mark Taylor, then the head of the Hot Wheels division, who first suggested the bus for the billboard project, lamenting that it was a shame the VW Bus was not more current. This only got Phil thinking about how to put a more "modern" twist on it, and the "drag bus-funny car style" theory was born. It was a far cry from his first sketch, which was shorter and tubbier. He began to draw several sketches to present to the senior managers at the next meeting.

The Bus was coming along on paper, but a lot of people felt the Bus wasn't "Hot Wheels enough," and that something a little more hot-rod oriented was needed. So, Phil drew another option to meet those prerequisites, and came up with a '30s panel truck (now known to collectors as the equally-popular Blown Delivery!) which was met with complete approval. It looked like the Bus was going to be put on the back-burner. However, Phil persisted.

At the next meeting, he made a copy of his Bus sketch and placed it on a board for showing, quickly coloring in the lines. He first showed the hot-rod option, then showed a three-quarter open view of the Bus. Once the bus sketch went up, everyone changed course and enthusiastically embraced it. The idea was at least going to leave the meeting room!

Phil would later say that, despite management approval, the Bus project still met with heavy obstacles. He sent a drawing to Asia, where it was instantly deemed too expensive to produce, with the equivalent of enough material in one bus to make three Hot Wheels cars! Phil had originally planned the engine to be plastic and vacuum metalized. The vendor operations changed it to die-cast metal due to a perceived safety issue with the exhaust pipes sticking out. There was concern that the pipes could be broken off, creating a hazard. When the first shots got back to Phil, the entire model was diecast. The finished casting was extremely heavy for a mainline car, weighing an estimated 114 grams, as opposed to other cars, which averaged 35 grams. Malaysia finally rejected the project, and it was moved to China. From that point, the Bus came to fruition, and was ready for issue.

Now, in order to convince management that it could be used for a 1996 First Editions release, marketing team member Jamie Wood suggested they could pack fewer in the cases. According to Phil, this was probably the saving grace for the Bus, advising that this was "pretty much the only way it made it through."

So, the Bus was released into the FE line, with the objective to relegate the casting to premium and promotional usage only after that run. This has mostly been the case, although the casting was supposed to make a brief return to the Mainline in the 2003 Preferred Series. After much ado, it was replaced by the 100% Microbus casting for retail purchase and the Bus was parlayed into a Toys 'R Us mail-in offer, with an orange and aqua variation. In 2010, the casting was modified as a T1 21 Window model with CoMolds and Real Riders, and made available in the "Phil's Garage" series. 4 color variations were issued. The T1 also made a 2013 appearance in the newly-released "Pop Culture" series, sporting a yellow and red body with "Flash Gordon" graphics. The standard Bus did make a brief return to retail in 2012 in the "Light Speeders" line, BUT...with a body made entirely of color-changing plastic. Not quite the same impact with Bus maniacs, but one most would add to their collection. Thankfully, in 2015, it came back in its full-blown metal glory as an M&M's model in the "Pop Culture" series.

In closing, unbeknownst to anyone, the VW Bus ended up being a collector favorite, although there are many who feel it is overrated/overused. The popularity was likely directly attributed to the cool design, and the craziness that was inspired by the short run back in 1996. Many collectors will say that the VW Bus is what got them back into the Hot Wheels hobby. Phil says that even Larry Wood predicted its success by uttering the now-famous phrase "Collectors are gonna be talking about that one for years." Good call, Larry! And kudos to Phil for providing the imagination and determination to make the Bus one of the most memorable castings in modern Hot Wheels history.

About This Guide

Each model from 1996-2015 has been meticulously researched with a sample sales average. Yes, there are going to be auctions where a particular model will go WELL OVER or even under the values quoted here. Average values don't account for all-out bidding skirmishes that take place among feverish collectors who insist on winning that model at any cost, or auctions that go unnoticed, due to poor verbiage. What I've done is take 12 auctions, high and low, and averaged them out to attain the value on the car. So, you may not have that skyrocketing value you're hoping for, but what you DO have is a solid *average* value that each car is currently selling for. The values reflected within will give you a very good idea of your buy/sell margins.

All values listed in this guide are for **Mint On Mint Card** (MOMC) examples. Just like any other collectible, there are certain things that can bring the value of any model down. Bent cards, dinged/collapsed blister, blister falling off the card, yellowing of the blister, color fading on the card, excessive scuff marks, etc. All are examples of deficiencies that will prevent any particular model from being considered MOMC. Take these into consideration when purchasing online. If the auction pictures are blurry, distant, dark…or just poor, in general…don't be afraid to ask the seller for better pictures. If the seller refuses to accommodate your request, then you've got a decision to make: Is it worth buying that item? VW Buses aren't generally the cheapest castings out there to collect! As any knowledgeable bus aficionado can attest to, some of the values can get downright INSANE. Always know every detail of what you're buying before committing to that purchase.

Lastly, no matter what, there is never going to be a "bible" for Hot Wheels values, regardless of technique. We can always get a target value, but nothing's ever exact. There will always be fluctuations in the hobby that affect values. That being said, I do believe that averaging out recent sales is a very good indicator of potential value, and I think this method will present itself well in this Guide. It's the same method I use for the price guide at NCHWA.com.

The Guide will include both incarnations of the Bus: The standard Drag Bus casting as well as the T1 Model. Yes, they're technically different castings altogether, but they're similar enough to include together in this issue. On a side note, the recently released C-3PO "Bus" has been included…it's labeled as a Drag Bus, but that's where the similarities end. It's been included for the fun of it, and because…well, Star Wars stuff is cool!

I wish you all the best with your collecting, and I'd like to thank you for purchasing the guide.

Neal Giordano

Neal Giordano
Founder/Editor, North Carolina Hot Wheels Association
Website: www.nchwa.com
Email: nchwa@yahoo.com

Year / Model	Description	Run #	Value
 1996 / First Edition	Collectors were scouring the pegs to find this one. A purely hypothetical run is rumored to be around 100K. It was immediately selling for $10.00 and up upon release, and was one of the catalysts that re-ignited the Hot Wheels phenomenon in 1996!	UNK	24.00
 1996 / Employee Christmas	**Top 25 Model (Ranked #1)** Given only to Mattel Employees in December of 1996, this one is rumored to be very limited at around 100. Other than the Santa tampos, there are no other details. There is a major concern with this issue, in that it was very easy to duplicate. One small way to authenticate it is by looking for a green roll cage.	100	2,650
 1997 / All Tune & Lube	The first promotional release of the VW Bus! Issued in August, 1997, the sporty flames on the sides made this one a big hit, since there were many collectors who never attained the '96 FE Bus. Oddly, the AT&L name does not appear anywhere on the blister card, or the bus itself. (This is a Liberty Promotions issued-bus)	25K	16.00
 1997 / J.C. Whitney	This bus had a limited run of 10K. For the longest time, it was the most limited Bus available to collectors, but has since been surpassed by several other releases, with runs of 10K or less. Can easily be found on the secondary today. Issued in a box, and not a blistercard.	10K	37.00

Year / Model	Description	Run #	Value

1997 / Internet I

The first Bus offering by Mattel via online exclusive. Rumored to be limited to a run of 10K, but this has been difficult to confirm. Great details, with all lights painted. Issued in a baggie, and not a blister card. — 10K — 25.00

1997 / Custom Car Designer

This one created quite a stir when it was issued! It marked the first time the bus was again available at a retail level! The run number is undetermined, but this one isn't considered rare. Ironically, it could be hard to find someday, since many thousands of them likely met their demise to customizers everywhere (value is for loose Bus only) — UNK — 13.00

1998 / 30th Anniversary

Same paint scheme as the 1996 First Edition model, except with a 30th Anniversary logo on the wing. It was issued in a box-type package, but the back of the blister card will definitely indicate that it's the 30th Anniversary model. — UNK — 19.00

1998 / Jiffy Lube

Issued in August, 1998. This bus doesn't have the Jiffy Lube name on it anywhere, but there is a JL sticker on the blister card. Limited to a run of 25K. Take a close look at the black Hot Wheels emblem on the side of this bus; curiously, it says "Hot Whee" instead of "Wheels." This error ran for the entire line! (This is a Liberty Promotions issued-bus) — 25K — 13.00

Year / Model	Description	Run #	Value
1998 / Van de Kamps	This green bus was a mail-in offer by VDK, and was limited to a run of 50K. You had to eat a TON of fish sticks to get this one! All lights are detailed, except for the signal lights on the front. The VW symbol was left unpainted.	50K	13.00
1998 / Blue Angels	This bus was the first of what was to be 4 military-themed buses marketed by M&D Toys and was limited to a run of 20K. F/A-18 Hornets make up the deco on the top and sides. Dedicated to the Navy's Blue Angels Flight Team, based in Pensacola, Florida.	20K	23.00
1998 / Thunderbirds	The second military-based theme to be issued. Marketed by M&D toys, and limited to a run of 30K. F-16 Fighting Falcons make up the deco on the top and sides. The Thunderbirds are based at Nellis AFB, Nevada.	30K	17.00
1999 / Navy SEALs	The third military-based theme to be issued. Marketed by M&D Toys, this bus is limited to a run of 30K. The headlights and signal lights are painted silver, while the VW symbol was left unpainted. Dedicated to the elite force based out of Virginia Beach (Naval Special Warfare group and its SEAL Teams 2, 4, 10 and 18)	30K	20.00

Year / Model	Description	Run #	Value
1999 / Golden Knights	The fourth and final military-based theme to be issued. Marketed by M&D Toys, this bus is limited to a run of 30K. Nicely detailed, with all lights painted. Tampos are based on the Army's elite parachute team, which is based at the home of the Airborne at Fort Bragg, North Carolina.	30K	16.00
1999 / Internet II	The second online exclusive offered at Mattel's website. Rumored to be limited to around 7K, but this has yet to be confirmed. Same details as the Internet I bus, but in a blue paint scheme. Issued in a baggie, along with a set of Revealers.	7K	20.00
1999 / Internet III	The third Internet exclusive from Mattel and limited to a run of 25K. This one took the longest to sell, finally being depleted in 2002 in a factory clearance. It was accompanied by a gold Sojourner Mars Rover model. Issued in a baggie.	25K	19.00
1999 / Malleco Tower Cranes	First rumored that only 8K were issued, but it's been difficult to accurately annotate the true number. Deep burgundy paint, and the First bus to use gold 5-spoke wheels. The Malleco Tower Cranes company is located in Portage, Indiana.	8K	16.00

Year / Model	Description	Run #	Value
1999 / Collector's Guide	The second VW Bus to be offered with Mattel software. Issued in celebration of the 30th Anniversary, this CD-ROM featured vast collector resources and pictures. First bus to use Redline tires. Unknown run number, but this one isn't considered rare in any way.	UNK	13.00
1999 / Mattel Vendor Operations Asia	**Top 25 Model (Ranked #2)** One of the rarest VW Buses ever made, limited to around 100. Issued in an acrylic plastic case with a green felt bottom. The MVOA bus displays incredibly well, and is the envy of Bus collectors everywhere. All emblems are water slide decals.	100	1,500
2001 / Penske (Black)	This bus sold out in two weeks. It was the first bus to utilize a wheel other than the standard 5-spoke wheels, by sporting a set of 6-spoke Pro Circuits. Also the first time that the Goodyear print appeared on the tires. (This is a Liberty Promotions issued-bus)	30K	14.00
2001 / Penske (Silver)	This silver version was inadvertently released early, supposedly in error. Nice change on the wheels, having utilized 5-spoke Mag wheels. (This is a Liberty Promotions issued-bus)	30K	14.00

Year / Model	Description	Run #	Value
 2001 / Penske (Red)	The red Penske bus was also released early, selling for large profits on eBay before finally becoming readily available. This was the 3rd and final issue in the Penske series (or, so we thought!) This is a Liberty Promotions-issued bus.	20K	14.00
 2001 / Penske (Burgundy)	**Top 25 Model (Ranked #4)** A small number of these pre-production models were shipped to Liberty Promotions. The color wasn't approved for sale, and the red bus was subsequently issued instead. However, it is believed that somewhere in the range of 50 of them were retained.	50	470.00
 2001 / 15th Annual Convention	Issued in October 2001 in Irvine, California. This was the first VW Bus to sport Real Riders. The model pictured at left is the correct version, with the yellow-tipped flame. The total run on this one is 6K, but there was an error/variation on the flame, which was limited to 2K.	4K	44.00
2001 / 15th Annual Convention	**Top 25 Model (Ranked #19)** This is the aforementioned 2K variation. Notice that the tip of the flame is red, and the yellow in the middle of the logo. Apparently, these were the first off the line, and approximately 2K were made before the variation was corrected.	2K	64.00

Year / Model	Description	Run #	Value
2002 / Hot Wheels Nationals	Issued by HWC.com, and made available at the Nationals in Reston, VA in April 2002. A total of 5K were available to attendees in Virginia, and another 5K were sold online at HWC.com, for a total run of 10K. The body features a chrome appearance, and pinstriping by Wayne Scott.	10K	26.00
2002 / M.A.C.E.	The now-defunct Midwest Air Cooled Enthusiasts Club (Wisconsin) teamed up with Mattel to offer this VW Bus in April, 2002. Limited to a run of 25K, this bus features 5-spoke Pro Circuits, with plastic Goodyear tires on the front and rear.	25K	14.00
2002 / Flying Customs	Issued by HWC.com in May of 2002. Limited to a run of 10K, this bus sold out in one day to Redline Club members. Great issue that reflects back on the 1975 Toy Fair era Super Van paint scheme, although the original had a "Flying Colors" tampo.	10K	26.00
2002 / Phil Riehlman 10th Ann.	**Top 25 Model (Ranked #13)** Issued at the 2nd Annual Hot Wheels Nationals held in Reston, Virginia, in honor of Phil's 10th Anniversary with Mattel. This bus features a Spectraflame orange paint job, foil decal on the blister and Convention logo on the roof (ltd. 400). There were a total of 5,012 issued, but in different variations	400	89.00

Year / Model	Description	Run #	Value
2002 / Phil Riehlman 10th Ann.	**Top 25 Model** (Ranked #19) Same description as original, but this one was issued with NO foil decal on the card, WITH the Convention logo on the roof (ltd. 1,900)	1,900	65.00
2002 / Phil Riehlman 10th Ann.	Same description as above, but this one was issued with NO foil decal or Convention logo on the roof (ltd. 2,712)	2,712	31.00
2002 / Phil Riehlman 10th Ann.	Issued in Summer of 2002, this Spectraflame blue bus is the follow-up to the orange Phil Riehlman bus Nationals. Limited to a run of 10K, this one was made available online, and sold out within a matter of hours. The tampo scheme is exactly the same as the orange version.	10k	29.00
2002 / Decades	Released in October of 2002 as a Target exclusive in a 10-car set, with decorator tin. Limited to a run of 25K. Very nice issue, with an off-white or pewter paint job, and a simple tampo on the side. Comes equipped with Redline Real Riders. **Value is for the loose bus by itself.**	25K	14.00

Year / Model	Description	Run #	Value
2003 / Toys "R" Us Mail-in	From the Preferred Series. Simple orange paint scheme with a white roof and silver wing. These were originally meant for a retail release, but they were replaced by the microbus late in the planning and attainable only by mail-in offer. Unknown run number.	UNK	15.00
2003 / Toys "R" Us Mail-in	From the Preferred Series. Simple aqua paint scheme with a white roof and silver wing. These were originally meant for a retail release, but they were replaced by the microbus late in the planning and attainable only by mail-in offer. Unknown run number.	UNK	13.00
2003 / HWC Flying Customs	Customized by David Chang and issued by HotWheelsCollectors.com. Features David's signature "Shredder" deco and 5-spoke Pro Circuits with "Kustom City" stamped in silver on the front and rear tires.	12,500	26.00
2003 / Flying Customs (Charity)	**Top 25 Model (Ranked #6)** Issued in 2003. Same tampo scheme as the chrome Flying Customs bus, but much more limited (1,000). Issued by HWC.com, with proceeds going to charity.	1K	307.00

Year / Model	Description	Run #	Value
2003 / Hall of Fame Series	**Top 25 Model** (Ranked #10) (Peterson Tour) Issued at the 17th Annual Collectors Convention on Sunday, October 5th, 2003. Easily recognizable with the Deora on the sides. Wheels are imprinted with "Hall of Fame" deco.	1,300	157.00
2004 / HWC Real Riders #6	This Real Riders bus features Spectraflame purple paint with a white roof, orange/yellow striping and 5-Spoke Goodyear Real Riders.	10,500	35.00
2004 / Lucky Charms	Issued in 2004 via mail-away offer from General Mills only. Features a red body with a yellow wing, Lucky Charms deco and 5-Spoke Goodyear wheels. Run number is undetermined, but these are definitely NOT rare. Many of them were likely chopped up for customs.	UNK	16.00
2004 / Wheaties	Issued in 2004 by mail-away offer from General Mills only. Features a light-blue body with an orange wing, Wheaties deco and 5-Spoke Goodyear wheels. Run number is undetermined.	UNK	13.00

Year / Model	Description	Run #	Value
2005 / Treasure Hunt	Issued as #13 in the 12-car Treasure Hunt Series, and available by mail-in only. There are bright and dark base variations, with no difference in value. There is also a card variation with a chrome decal indicating it's from a Factory Set (add approx. $10.00 to the standard TH value for this one)	UNK	46.00
2005 / Treasure Hunt	NOTE: This is NOT a legitimate Osaka show issue, as the Dairy Delivery was the official model. Apparently, some decals came up missing, and a few appeared on the Treasure Hunt Bus. Do NOT pay more for this one than you would for the standard TH model!	UNK	46.00
2005 / HWC Real Riders	Real Riders Series 4. Simple graphics allow the purple Spectraflame paint to shine through. #5 on the sides, with chrome 5-Spoke Redline Real Rider tires.	11K	23.00
2005 / RLC "Thank You"	Issued in 2005 by HWC.com for its Redline Club members. Chrome roof and red Spectraflame paint. The deco is made up entirely of decals. Issued with Redline Real Riders.	14,472	27.00

Year / Model	Description	Run #	Value
2005 / Mongoose	Issued with the Mongoose & Snake Drag Set by HWC.com. Features a red body with white roof, "Mongoose" racing deco and Goodyear rear/5-Spoke front tires. Definite nod to the Snake & Mongoose days, back in the 70's. (Value is for the bus only)	10K	24.00
2005 / Snake	Issued with the Mongoose & Snake Drag Set by HWC.com. Features a yellow body with white roof, "Snake" racing deco and Goodyear rear/5-Spoke front tires. Definite nod to the Snake & Mongoose days, back in the 70's. (Value is for the bus only)	10K	28.00
2006 HWC Real Riders	Real Riders Series 5. This model has a Spectraflame teal body with a white roof, black wing, light-blue flame deco on the sides and chrome hub 5-Spoke Goodyear Real Riders.	11K	33.00
2006 / RLC NEO Classics	Club Exclusive. This model has a Spectraflame red body with #6/racing deco on the sides, white striping, "Neo Classics" tampo and chrome hub 5-Spoke Redline Real Riders.	13,775	26.00

Year / Model	Description	Run #	Value
2006 / Mystery Car	Issued in recognition of the 10th anniversary of the VW Bus. Mystery Car 5 of 5. "Ten Year Anniversary" is printed in red on the Real Rider tires. The body is chrome and red, with a black roof. VW logo on the roof also has "10th Anniversary Hot Wheels VW Bus" and "1996-2006" printed around it.	UNK	28.00
2007 / HWC Real Riders	One of only 3 Mattel buses issued in 2007. Spectraflame orange with black stripe extending past the windows and ghost flames. 5-Spoke Real Rider tires with "Goodyear" printed on them.	11K	30.00
2007 / Osaka Convention	**Top 25 Model** (Ranked #23) Sold to RLC members through the HWC website, this bus sold out quickly online. Black body with ice blue flames & Real Rider wheels/tires that have Phillip Riehlman printed on them.	4K	53.00
2007 / Osaka Convention	Sold in commemoration of the 2007 Osaka, Japan HWC show on May 27th, 2007. This model is paired with a similarly-marked VW Drag Truck in an acrylic case. (Value is for the complete set)	4K	129.00

Year / Model	Description	Run #	Value
2008 / Los Angeles Convention	Issued in 2008 for the 22nd Hot Wheels Collector's Convention in Los Angeles, California. Spectraflame dark blue with blue outlined flames on the sides, black wing and convention logo on the roof. 5-Spoke Real Rider tires.	3K	36.00
2008 / Since '68	Issued as #1 in a set of 40. Metalflake green body with grey flames on the sides and roof. Redline Basic Wheels up front; rear wheels are Redline standard VW Bus wheels.	UNK	31.00
2008 / 40 Years of Hot Wheels	Issued in a set, this bus is a nod to its 1996 predecessor, as it sports the exact same tampo scheme, albeit with a matte, primer blue paint on the body. Standard 5-Spoke VW Bus wheels on front.	UNK	23.00
2008 / Top 40	Issued as part of a Wal-Mart set, this bus features a pearlescent yellow paint job with yellow and grey flames on the roof and sides. Comes with standard Redline VW Bus wheels.	UNK	15.00

Year / Model	Description	Run #	Value
2008 / Mexico Convention	Issued in 2008 for the first-ever Hot Wheels Collector's Convention in Mexico on September 6-7. The show version features a sticker on the front of the blister pack. Bus is gold chrome with a black roof. Orange and green flames on the sides, with the Hot Wheels logo, and standard Redline VW Bus Wheels.	3K	37.00
2008 / Mexico Convention	Same description as Show edition, but WITHOUT the sticker on the blister card. Bus is gold chrome with a black roof. Orange and green flames on the sides, with the Hot Wheels logo, and standard Redline VW Bus Wheels.	UNK	35.00
2008 / HWC Real Riders	Issued as #1 of 6 in the series. Features a deep gold chrome paint job with a red, yellow and white version of the Hot Wheels logo on the sides. Produced with chrome 5-Spoke Redline Real Riders.	10K	34.00
2008 / Redline Poker Club	**Top 25 Model (Ranked #3)** Event VW Bus issued by Mattel in conjunction with the annual poker tournament played at the 2008 California Convention. Features a black body with white roof and pinstriping deco by Wayne Scott. Issued with 5-spoke Redline wheels.	72	710.00

Year / Model	Description	Run #	Value
 2009 / Redline Club (Police)	**Top 25 Model** (Ranked #17) Issued as 1 of 4 RLC club cars. Bus features a black paint job, with a white roof. The most noticeable feature is the red & blue light bar on the roof; a first for the Bus. Produced with Replica Redline (Neo) wheels. Issued with a button and a Larry Wood poster.	4K	66.00
 2009 / Redline Club (Fire)	**Top 25 Model** (Ranked #20) Issued as 2 of 4 RLC club cars. Bus features a red Spectraflame paint job, with white inset and black ghost flames. The most noticeable feature is the red light bar on the roof; a first for the Bus. Produced with Replica Redline (Neo) wheels. Issued with a button and a Larry Wood poster.	5K	62.00
 2009 / Redline Club (Military)	**Top 25 Model** (Ranked #24) Issued as 3 of 4 RLC club cars. Bus features a dark olive green Spectraflame paint job with a flat black roof. The most noticeable feature is the red & blue light bar on the roof; a first for the Bus. Produced with Replica Redline (Neo) wheels. Issued with a button and a Larry Wood poster.	6K	53.00
 2009 / Redline Club (Taxi)	**Top 25 Model** (Ranked #21) Issued in as 4 of 4 RLC club cars. Bus features a yellow/gold Spectraflame paint job with a gloss black roof. The most noticeable feature is the amber light bar on the roof; a first for the Bus. Produced with Replica Redline (Neo) wheels. Issued with a button and a Larry Wood poster.	7K	61.00

Year / Model	Description	Run #	Value
2009 / Los Angeles Convention	Issued as #1 of 4 in the Convention Series. Features white/blue body with blue flame deco, convention logo, light bar on the roof and 5-spoke hubs with Real Riders.	3K	35.00
2009 / Mattel Employee Christmas	**Top 25 Model (Ranked #5)** Chrome body with white "ghost" flames, "Happy Holidays" deco on doors and metallic red 5-Spoke hubs with white Real Riders. Given to Mattel employees only.	2K	360.00
2010 / Phil's Garage (T1)	T1 body style, introduced in 2010. Chase version with signature on base, issued in a Wal*Mart exclusive 30-car set. Re-tooled version of the original VW Drag Bus, adding roof contours and vents, along with the windows added on the side panels. Blue body with a silver top. Grey/chrome CoMolds are the standard tire.	UNK	17.00
2010 / Phil's Garage (T1)	T1 body style, available at retail. Grey/black body with a molded top. Grey/chrome CoMolds are the standard tire. (Add $2.00 for signed chase versions)	UNK	11.00

Year / Model	Description	Run #	Value

2010 / Phil's Garage (T1)

T1 body style, available at retail. Orange/black body with a molded top. Grey/chrome CoMolds are the standard tire. (Add $2.00 for signed chase versions) — UNK — 12.00

2010 / Phil's Garage (T1)

T1 body style, available at retail. Black/white body with a molded top. Grey/chrome CoMolds are the standard tire. (Add $2.00 for signed chase versions) — UNK — 12.00

2010 / Brazil Convention

Top 25 Model (Ranked #22)
Issued for the Brazil Hot Wheels Convention in 2010. Features green, white and yellow body, with green flames, and "Brazil" on the wing. Green 5spk Real Riders are standard. — 5K — 60.00

2010 / Los Angeles Convention

Issued for the 24th Collectors Convention, held in Los Angeles, California from October 13th-17th. Body is red and white, with orange/yellow flames on the side, and the convention logo on the roof. Chrome 5spk Real Riders are standard. — 3,500 — 29.00

Year / Model	Description	Run #	Value
2010 / Dream Halloween	**Top 25 Model (Ranked #14)** Issued to those who supported the "Children With Aids" foundation. Metalflake orange body with "Drag-O-Lantern" on the sides and Real Rider tires with green chrome 5-Spoke hubs.	2K	85.00
2010 / Japan Custom Car Show	**Top 25 Model (Ranked #16)** Issued with a similarly-marked VW Fastback. Was supposed to be sold at the Japan show in 2010, but never made it overseas. Sets were later sold as an RLC special for $39.99 in November, 2011. Bus features deco by Phil Riehlman, a white/black body with red front and 5-Spoke Redline Real Riders.	1,500	80.00
2010 / Japan Custom Car Show	**Top 25 Model (Ranked #8)** Issued with a similarly-marked VW Fastback. Was supposed to be sold at the Japan show, but never made it overseas. Sets were later sold as an RLC special for $59.99 in November, 2011. Bus features deco by Phil Riehlman, a white/black body with orange front and 5-Spoke Yellowline Real Riders.	500	194.00
2011 / Collector's Nationals	Issued during the 11th Annual Nationals held in Cincinnati, Ohio on April 13th-17th. This T1-style VW Bus is burgundy and off-white, with orange/red flames on the side, and the convention logo on the roof. Limited to a run of 3,500 and issued with chrome 5-Spoke Real Riders.	3,500	38.00

Year / Model	Description	Run #	Value
2011 / K-Mart Mail-In	This was the 3rd mail-in offer for 2011, and could be obtained by sending 20 cardbacks of qualifying models between 9/17-10/17 2011, along with receipts. Features gold chrome paint, dark red/white flames on the sides/top and 5-Spoke Redline Real Rider tires. Unknown run number.	UNK	26.00
2011 / Los Angeles Convention	A T1 model that was issued during the 25th Convention held on Oct. 5th-9th, 2011. Metalflake black top with white lower half, convention logo on the roof and "Collector's Convention" with striping on the sides. 5-Spoke Real Rider wheels.	3,500	32.00
2011 / Convention Finale	**Top 25 Model (Ranked #7)** Issued during the 25th Convention Finale to paid ticketholders. Rumored to be limited to 1,500, but there were only 1,100 attendees. Bus is Spectraflame pink, with the convention logo on the roof, "Thank You" on the wing and flames on the sides.	1,500	210.00
2011 / HW Garage	Issued in the Garage 30-Car set in 2011. Features flat-black paint with "Drag Bus" striping deco on the roof and sides. Issued with red hub 5-Spoke Whitewall Real Riders. Unknown run #.	UNK	24.00

Year / Model	Description	Run #	Value
2012 / RLC Subscription	**Top 25 Model** (Ranked #11) Issued as the 13th car to 2011 RLC Subscription holders in a bonus tin storage box. Features Spectraflame antifreeze paint, green/white flame striping deco on the sides and a white plastic top. Issued with Redline Neo wheels. (Value is for bus by itself, not the tin)	2K	115.00
2012 / Mexico Convention	Issued at the 5th Collector's Convention in Mexico that was held on August 31 through September 2nd. Features black & white body with a silver roof, "Mexico" on the wing, "5A Convencion" logo on the sides and chrome hub Real Riders (5-Spoke Mags on rear)	4K	35.00
2012 / Light Speeders	Available at retail, this model features an orange plastic body that would temporarily hold template and other designs when the special light was applied. The light casing came in two different colors: pink and grey. The metal chassis is mounted with 5-Spoke wheels. Unknown run number, but this model is not considered rare.	UNK	6.00
 2012 / 26th Annual Convention	Issued at the 26th Convention in Garden Grove, CA, held from Oct 3-7, commemorating 12 years of design by Mike McClone. The bus features a black/white body with flame deco was designed by McClone, and the 26th Convention logo, which was designed by Steve Vandervate. The wheels are chrome 5-Spoke mags, with Real Riders. Limited to 2K, with a dinner issue (next page) being limited to 500.	2K	35.00

Year / Model	Description	Run #	Value
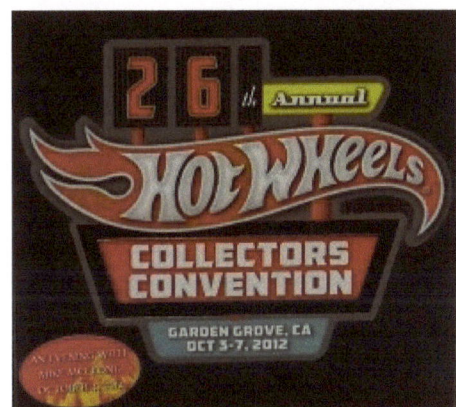 2012 / 26th Annual Convention	**Dinner Edition**. (The Dinner issue will have a sticker on the front of the card that says "An evening with Mike McClone, October 4, 2012.") Issued at the 26th Convention in Garden Grove, CA, held from Oct 3-7, commemorating 12 years of design by Mike McClone. Same features as the standard Convention Bus.	500	47.00
 2012 / Japan Convention	**Top 25 Model (Ranked #12)** Issued at the 2012 Convention in Yokohama, Japan on Dec.12, 2012 commemorating artwork by Hiro "Wildman" Ishii, who was mentored by Ed "Big Daddy" Roth himself. The bus features a black/yellow body with chrome 5-Spoke mags. Limited to 1,500 total, but there is a right-facing packaging variation that was limited to 300.	1,200	115.00
 2012 / Japan Convention	**Top 25 Model (Ranked #9)** **Facing right in package**. Same details as the standard Convention Bus above, but limited to only 300 facing this direction.	300	190.00
 2013 / Pop Culture	Issued in the Pop Culture series (King Features segment). This T1 model features a vibrant yellow and red body with "Flash Gordon deco, and chrome 5-Spoke mag hubs with Redline Real Riders. It was available at retail, but this Bus has an unknown run number. It isn't considered rare, by any means.	UNK	12.00

Year / Model	Description	Run #	Value
2013 / 13th Collector Nationals	Issued for the 13th Collector Nationals that took place from April 10-14 in Indianapolis, Indiana. Features a convention logo on the roof, "Race Team Security" on the wing, a light bar with blue/red "lights", white/blue body with HW Race Team deco and chrome hub 5-Spoke Mag hubs with "Hoosier" Real Riders	3K	45.00
2013 / RLC – HWC.com	A T1 model that was issued via online sale on July 16, 2013. This issue sold out within 45 minutes! Features a Spectraflame blue body with a white roof, Hot Wheels Racing tampos and chrome 5-Spoke Mag hubs with "GoodYear" Real Rider tires. Despite the successful sell-out, this sale was marred by major issues from the website's servers.	4K	34.00
2013 / 27th Annual Convention	This bus was issued during the 27th Annual Hot Wheels Collectors Convention in Garden Grove, California, held on Sept. 25-29, 2013. The body is blue with dark/light blue flame/pinstripe deco and the 27th Annual Convention logo on the wing. The wheels are chrome 5-Spoke Mags, with Real Riders.	4K	37.00
2013 / K-Mart Mail-In	This was the 4th mail-in offer for 2013, and could be obtained by sending 20 cardbacks of qualifying models along with receipts. This model features Spectraflame pink/matte black paint, Hot Wheels deco on the sides and 5-Spoke (rear) Redline Real Rider tires. Unknown run number.	UNK	25.00

Year / Model	Description	Run #	Value
2013 / Color Shifters	Released in 2013, this plastic-bodied bus features a green-to-white color change when submerged in water. The metal base is accompanied by chrome hub Open-Hole 5-Spoke wheels. This bus is not limited in any way, and averaged just under $4.00 at retail.	UNK	7.00
2014 / Pop Culture	A T-1 model that features vibrant Foghorn Leghorn graphics, and "Looney Tunes" on the wing. The wheels are 5-Spoke Mag hubs with Redline Real Riders. Unknown run number, but not considered rare.	UNK	11.00
2014 / 28th Annual Convention	This T1 model was released for the April 1, 2014 Collector's Convention in Oak Brook, Illinois. It has an orange body with a white roof, white swirl tampos and mag hub Real Riders with "Oak Brook" lettering. Limited to a run of 2,400.	2,400	30.00
2014 / Redline Club (Gulf Racing)	**Top 25 Model (Ranked #18)** This bus is technically a 2013 HWC issue, but due to some issues, it wasn't actually released until Dec, 2014. Metallic aqua/orange body with Gulf deco and 5-Spoke Mag hubs on Firestone Real Riders.	4K	65.00

Year / Model	Description	Run #	Value
 2015/ Pop Culture (Mars Candies)	This was the first non-T1 issue to see a retail run since 2011! Yellow body with brown roof, M&M deco and Redline Real Riders with 5-Spoke Mag hubs. Unknown run #, but this one was initially very difficult find at the retail level.	UNK	10.00
 2015 / Star Wars (C-3PO)	Since I love most things Star Wars, I included this one for the fun of it. This is technically NOT a Drag bus, but…it's labeled as such. It's a pretty cool version of C-3PO! (Issued in 2 pack with R2-D2 and on a single blister)	UNK	8.00

Liberty Promotions, Inc. specializes in designing and producing die-cast vehicles for businesses and organizations. Located in Lewisville, Texas, the company has been in business since 1993. Liberty is probably best-known for its prolific use of the VW Bus casting, having issued over 100 since first releasing the All Tune & Lube Bus in 1997 (this was also the first-ever promotional release of the VW Bus!) Utilizing creative and highly-detailed graphics, Liberty's Bus issues have become the stuff of legend over the years.

Year / Model	Description	Run #	Value
2002/ Charity VW Bus	Issued in May of 2002 in memoriam of the September 11 tragedies in 2001. Proceeds were donated to 1 of 4 different charities that collectors could choose from. This blue wing version is limited to 1,500. NOTE: Comes with a Certificate of Authenticity that is serial numbered and watermarked.	1,500	40.00
2002/ Charity VW Bus	Same information as above, but the Red wing version was far more limited, with a run of only 500. NOTE: Comes with a Certificate of Authenticity that is serial numbered and watermarked.	500	70.00
2003 / Kruizinwagon	Issued in December of 2003. Commissioned by Indian Automotive of Sydney, Australia. Aluminum enamel finish, with ghost flames and Goodyear Real Rider tires. Regular Run was 900, while the Rebel Run or "chase" version was 100. Rebel Run issue had a small kangaroo tampo on the rear quarter panels.	900 100	66.00 150.00

Year / Model	Description	Run #	Value
2003 / Kruizinwagon	Same information as aluminum issue. Black matte finish, with ghost flames and Goodyear Real Rider tires. Regular Run was 900, while the Rebel Run or "chase" version was 100. Rebel Run issue had a small kangaroo tampo on the rear quarter panels.	900 100	50.00 150.00
2004 / Dallas Convention	**Midnight**. Issued in April of 2004 to commemorate the first-ever Hot Wheels Nationals being held in Texas. Midnight blue with rubber Goodyear Real Riders. 250 were sold at the convention, and the remainder were sold online. Regular run was 1,125, while the Rebel Run or "chase" version was 125. Rebel Run issue has a small armadillo on it.	1,125 125	39.00 113.00
2004 / Dallas Convention	**Sunrise**. Same information as above. Metallic rust with rubber Goodyear Real Riders. 250 were sold at the convention, and the remainder were sold online. Regular run was 1,125, while the Rebel Run or "chase" version was 125. Rebel Run issue has a small armadillo on it.	1,125 125	44.00 118.00
2004 / Sturgis Set (Gal)	Issued in August, 2004 as a set, accompanied by a chopper. Metallic "Buffalo" Brown with the official Sturgis Rally Logo. Chrome 5-Spoke deep dish wheels with rubber "Goodyear" tires. Regular run was 1,300, while the Rebel Run or "chase" version was 200. Rebel Run issue is Metallic "Forest" Green.	1,300 200	44.00 99.00

Year / Model	Description	Run #	Value
2004 / Sturgis Set (Guy)	Issued in August, 2004 as a set, accompanied by a chopper. Metallic "Buffalo" Brown with the official Sturgis Rally Logo. Chrome 5-Spoke deep dish wheels with rubber "Goodyear" tires. Regular run was 1,300, while the Rebel Run or "chase" version was 200. Rebel Run issue is Metallic "Forest" Green.	1,300 200	44.00 99.00
2004 / Halloween	**Graveyard**. Issued in October, 2004. High-gloss Spooky Purple Paint. Issued with two shades of purple, (38% light and 62% dark), but this isn't considered in the value. Regular run was 2,500, while the Rebel Run or "chase" version was 500. Rebel Run issue is the "cat" version.	2,500 500	35.00 60.00
2004 / Volks-Drag'n	**Hot Shot Pink**. Issued in November, 2004. Pink paint deco represents a "funny bus" dragster look from the late '60s/early '70s era, with aluminum sideskirts and wing. Regular run was 1,300, while the Rebel Run or "chase" version was 200. Rebel Run issue has white sideskirts and wing.	1,300 200	34.00 68.00
2004 / Drag-On Wagon	**Radioactive Green**. Issued in November, 2004. Green paint deco represents a "funny bus" dragster look from the late '60s/early '70s era, with aluminum sideskirts and wing. Regular run was 1,300, while the Rebel Run or "chase" version was 200. Rebel Run issue has white sideskirts and wing.	1,300 200	33.00 52.00

Year / Model	Description	Run #	Value
2005 / Collection Builder	**Electric Orange**. Issued in February, 2005. Orange paint with silver wing, and graphics by Dave Chang. Regular run was 1,300, while the Rebel Run or "chase" version was 200. Rebel Run issue is changed to a steel or aluminum body color, with the same graphics.	1,300 200	36.00 85.00
2005 / Collection Builder	**Cobalt Blue**. Issued in February, 2005. Blue paint with silver wing, and graphics by Dave Chang. Regular run was 1,300, while the Rebel Run or "chase" version was 200. Rebel Run issue is changed to a steel or aluminum body color, with the same graphics.	1,300 200	32.00 85.00
2005 / Pirates of the Caribbean	**Pirate's Treasure**. Issued in May, 2005. "Sea Foam" or aqua body paint and pirate graphics. Regular run was 1,300, while the Rebel Run or "chase" version was 200. Rebel Run issue is changed to a "booty gold" body color, with the same graphics.	1,300 200	25.00 71.00
2005 / Pirates of the Caribbean	**Scourge of the Sea**. Issued in May, 2005. Black Pearl body paint and pirate graphics. Regular run was 1,300, while the Rebel Run or "chase" version was 200. Rebel Run issue is changed to a "booty gold" body color, with the same graphics.	1,300 200	31.00 65.00

Year / Model	Description	Run #	Value
2005 / Sturgis Set (Gal)	Issued in July, 2005 as a set, accompanied by a matching chopper. Metallic magenta with the official Sturgis Rally Logo. Regular run was 1,300, while the Rebel Run or "chase" version was 200. Rebel Run issue is changed to a glossy black body color, with the same graphics.	1,300 200	36.00 59.00
2005 / Sturgis Set (Guy)	Issued in July, 2005 as a set, accompanied by a matching chopper. Metallic copper with the official Sturgis Rally Logo. Regular run was 1,300, while the Rebel Run or "chase" version was 200. Rebel Run issue is changed to a glossy black body color, with the same graphics.	1,300 200	35.00 66.00
2005 / Halloween	**Witch**. Issued in October, 2005. "Pitch Black" paint with spooky witch graphics. Regular run was 1,300, while the Rebel Run or "chase" version was 200. Rebel Run issue is changed to a ZAMAC or "bare" look, with the same graphics.	1,300 200	32.00 65.00
2005 / Halloween	**Dungeon**. Issued in October, 2005. "Pitch Black" paint with spooky dungeon graphics. Regular run was 1,300, while the Rebel Run or "chase" version was 200. Rebel Run issue is changed to a ZAMAC or "bare" look, with the same graphics.	1,300 200	41.00 73.00

Year / Model	Description	Run #	Value
2006 / Surfin' Series #1 	**Wave Rider**. Issued in April, 2006. Sky blue paint with surfing and beach graphics. Two surfboards are mounted to the roof. Regular run was 1,300, while the Rebel Run or "chase" version was 200. Rebel Run issue is changed to a "Sun Yellow" body paint with the same graphics.	1,300 200	38.00 85.00
2006 / Surfin' Series #2	**Woodie**. Issued in April, 2006. Cream/tan paint with surfing and mock woodgrain side panels and surfshop stickers. Two surfboards are mounted to the roof. Regular run was 1,300, while the Rebel Run or "chase" version was 200. Rebel Run issue is changed to a maroon/burgundy body paint with the same graphics.	1,300 200	39.00 71.00
2006 / Cops & Robbers 	**Robbers**. Issued in May, 2006. Matte grey paint job, with simple gunmen graphics. Regular run was 1,300, while the Rebel Run or "chase" version was 200. Rebel Run issue is changed to black and white body paint with the same graphics.	1,300 200	25.00 66.00
2006 / Cops & Robbers	**Cops**. Issued in May, 2006. Blue and white paint job, with simple police graphics. Regular run was 1,300, while the Rebel Run or "chase" version was 200. Rebel Run issue is changed to black and white body paint with the same graphics.	1,300 200	29.00 78.00

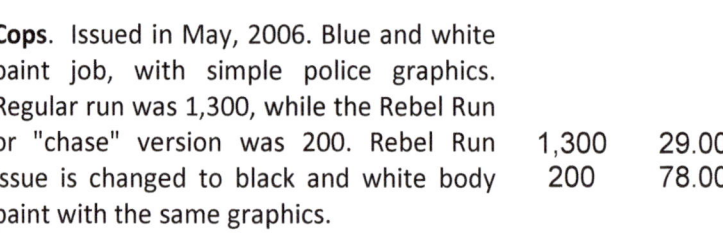

Year / Model	Description	Run #	Value
2006 / Pirates of the Caribbean 2	**Blackbeard's Revenge**. Issued in July, 2006. "Revenge Red" paint job, with skull and crossbones/pirate graphics. The headlights have skulls on them. There were two Rebel Run issues for this model: the regular run is 1,000, while Rebel Run #1 is Sterling silver plated, and limited to 150. Rebel Run #2 is 24-Karat gold plated, and limited to 50. Graphics remained the same on all.	1,300 150 50	38.00 125.00 650.00
2006 / Pirates of the Caribbean 2	**Captain Kidd's Treasure**. Issued in July, 2006. Midnight Black paint job, with skull and crossbones/pirate graphics. There were two Rebel Run issues for this model: the regular run is 1,000, while Rebel Run #1 is Sterling silver plated, and limited to 150. Rebel Run #2 is 24-Karat gold plated, and limited to 50. Graphics remained the same on all.	1,300 150 50	38.00 142.00 600.00
2006 / Fire & Ice	**Fire**. Issued in August, 2006. "Fire Red" paint job, with Warrior and dragon graphics. The regular run is 1,300, while the Rebel Run version is limited to 200. Rebel Run issue is changed to a "Charcoal Black" body and limited to 200. Graphics remained the same on both.	1,300 200	24.00 82.00
2006 / Fire & Ice	**Ice**. Issued in August, 2006. "Arctic Ice" paint job, with Viking graphics. The regular run is 1,300, while the Rebel Run version is limited to 200. Rebel Run issue is changed to a chrome body and limited to 200. Graphics remained the same on both.	1,300 200	28.00 88.00

Year / Model	Description	Run #	Value
2006 / Halloween	**Frankenstein**. Issued in October, 2006. Chrome body with Frankenstein/Mad Scientist graphics. The regular run is 1,300, while the Rebel Run version is limited to 200. Rebel Run issue is changed to a blue chrome body and limited to 200. Graphics remained the same on both.	1,300 200	25.00 53.00
2006 / Halloween	**Vampire**. Issued in October, 2006. "Blood Red" paint on the body with Dracula/victim graphics. The regular run is 1,300, while the Rebel Run version is limited to 200. Rebel Run issue is changed to a red chrome body and limited to 200. Graphics remained the same on both.	1,300 200	35.00 102.00
2006 / Fighter Bus	**P-40 Flying Tiger**. Issued in November, 2006. Green and tan camouflage with P-40/fighter plane graphics. The regular run is 1,300, while the Rebel Run version is limited to 200. Rebel Run issue is changed to white winter camouflage and limited to 200. Graphics remained the same on both.	1,300 200	35.00 70.00
2006 / Bomber Bus	**B-17 Yankee Gal**. Issued in November, 2006. Aluminum paint with "Yankee Gal" graphics. The regular run is 1,300, while the Rebel Run version is limited to 200. Rebel Run issue is changed to "Military Green" and limited to 200. Graphics remained the same on both.	1,300 200	30.00 117.00

Year / Model	Description	Run #	Value
2007 / Alien Bus	**Autopsy**. Issued in January, 2007. Glow-in-the-Dark green paint with alien graphics. There were two Rebel Run issues for this model: the regular run is 1,000, while Rebel Run #1 is "Day-Glo Orange", and limited to 300. Rebel Run #2 is "Bone White" with glow-in-the-dark graphics, and limited to 200. Graphics remained the same on all.	1,000 300 200	26.00 82.00 95.00
2007 / Alien Bus	**Abduction**. Issued in January, 2007. Glow-in-the-Dark green paint with alien graphics. There were two Rebel Run issues for this model: the regular run is 1,000, while Rebel Run #1 is "Day-Glo Orange", and limited to 300. Rebel Run #2 is "Bone White" with glow-in-the-dark graphics, and limited to 200. Graphics remained the same on all.	1,000 300 200	30.00 75.00 86.00
2007 Surfin' Series 3	**Fire Woodie**. Issued in February, 2007. Black paint with faux woodgrain sides and flames, along with two flamed surfboards on the roof & Hawaiian surf deco. The regular run is 1,300, while the Rebel Run version is limited to 200. Rebel Run issue is changed to dark silver paint. Graphics remained the same on both.	1,300 200	34.00 108.00
2007 Surfin' Series 3	**Freaky Tiki**. Issued in February, 2007. Purple and orange paint with Stone Gods and Headhunter graphics. The regular run is 1,300, while the Rebel Run version is limited to 200. Rebel Run issue has the purple and orange flipped around. Graphics remained the same on both.	1,300 200	31.00 84.00

Year / Model	Description	Run #	Value
2007 / Speedwagon 1	Issued in July, 2007. Checkerboard paint scheme with Liberty Legion logo, red muscle car & blue dragster. The regular run is 1,000, while Rebel Run version #1 is limited to 350 ("Diecast X" logo on roof). Rebel Run version #2 is limited to 350 (RIHWC logo on roof)	1,000 350 350	33.00 58.00 56.00
2007 / Speedwagon 2	Issued in July, 2007. Checkerboard paint scheme with Liberty 100th logo, Red Baron & blue coupe. The regular run is 1,000, while the Rebel Run version #1 is limited to 350 (Liberty Legion logo on roof). Rebel Run version #2 is limited to 350 (Mexico club logo on roof.)	1,000 350 350	37.00 60.00 104.00
2007 / Halloween	**Jack-'O-Lantern**. Issued in October, 2007. "Glowing Orange" paint, with Halloween/Jack-o-Lantern graphics on sides and roof. The regular run is 1,300, while the Rebel Run version is limited to 200. The Rebel Run issue has alternate pumpkin graphics and "Rebel Run" text on the roof.	1,300 200	29.00 84.00
2007 / Pirates of The Caribbean 3	**Sneak Attack**. Issued in December, 2007. "Green Mist" paint job, with skeleton pirate graphics. There were two Rebel Run issues for this model: the regular run is 1,300, while Rebel Run #1 is Sterling silver plated, and limited to 150. Rebel Run #2 is 24-Karat gold plated, and limited to 50. Graphics remained the same on all.	1,300 150 50	25.00 122.00 750.00

Year / Model	Description	Run #	Value
2007 / Pirates of the Caribbean 3	**Mutineer Bay**. Issued in December, 2007. "Dark Rum" paint job, with skeleton pirate and map graphics. There were two Rebel Run issues for this model: the regular run is 1,300, while Rebel Run #1 is Sterling silver plated, and limited to 150. Rebel Run #2 is 24-Karat gold plated, and limited to 50. Graphics remained the same on all.	1,300 150 50	25.00 138.00 680.00
2008 / Surfin' Series 5	**Bamboozled**. Issued in March, 2008. Cherry paneling, oak paneling, and bamboo trim cover the entire bus. Two surfboards with bamboo deco are mounted to the roof. Regular run was 1,300, while the Rebel Run or "chase" version was 200. Rebel Run issue is changed to "Bamboozled Burnt" body paint with the same graphics.	1,300 200	29.00 72.00
2008 / Surfin' Series 6	**Shark Attack.** Issued in March, 2008. "Deep Ocean Blue" and light blue paint with a Great White on the port side, and Hammerheads on the starboard. Two surfboards are mounted to the roof. Regular run was 1,300, while the Rebel Run or "chase" version was 200. Rebel Run issue has a black roof and black side skirts.	1,300 200	31.00 81.00
2008 / Chicago Nationals	**Gangster.** Issued in April, 2008 to commemorate the Hot Wheels Collectors Nationals in Chicago. "Asphalt Black" paint with gangster/city graphics. Regular run was 1,300, while the Rebel Run or "chase" version was 400. Rebel Run issue is changed to the "Al Capone Edition." (Al Capone is pictured on the right rear side panel)	1,300 400	27.00 48.00

Year / Model	Description	Run #	Value
2008 / Chicago Nationals	Issued in April, 2008 to commemorate the Collectors Nationals in Chicago. "Glossy Black" paint with graphics of the Great Chicago Fire of 1871. Regular run was 1,300, while the Rebel Run or "chase" version was 400. Rebel Run issue changed to the "Mrs. O'Leary's Cow" Edition. Graphics remained the same, but with a small cow graphic on the upper right rear end.	1,300 400	24.00 68.00
2008 / Super Flames 1	**Blazin' Bus**. Issued in May, 2008. Blue paint with orange/red/yellow flame graphics. Regular run was 1,300, while the Rebel Run or "chase" version was 200. The Rebel Run issue is changed to chrome body. Graphics remained the same.	1,300 200	22.00 80.00
2008 / Sturgis Set	Issued in July, 2008. Matte black paint with motorcycle and flame graphics. Issued with a matching motorcycle. Regular run was 1,300, while the Rebel Run or "chase" version was 200. The Rebel Run issue is changed to chrome body. Graphics remained the same.	1,300 200	34.00 114.00
2008 / Summer Smash	Issued in August, 2008 in commemoration of Summer Smash, held in Warwick, Rhode Island. "Mellow Yellow" paint with sunburst graphics. Regular run was 1,300, and there were two Rebel Run or "chase" versions. The first Rebel Run is limited to 250 and features a gold chrome body, while Rebel Run number 2 is also limited to 250, featuring a metallic gold body. Graphics remained the same on all.	1,300 250 250	23.00 45.00 45.00

Year / Model	Description	Run #	Value
2008 / Halloween	**Zombie**. Issued in September, 2008. "Radioactive Slime" (green) paint with zombie graphics, and HAZMAT symbol on headlights. Regular run was 1,300, while the Rebel Run or "chase" version was 200. The Rebel Run issue is changed to "Contaminated Slime" (black) paint. Graphics remained the same.	1,300 200	26.00 88.00
2008 / Route 66	Issued in October, 2008. Black paint scheme with Route 66 graphics, with a '57 Desoto and '58 Ford on the sides. Regular run was 1,300, while the Rebel Run or "chase" version was 200. The Rebel Run issue is changed to a white wing, with the number "66" printed on it. Graphics remained the same.	1,300 200	35.00 89.00
2009 / Lightning Wagon	Issued in December, 2008. Deep Purple paint scheme with lavender glow lightning bolt graphics. Regular run was 1,300, while the Rebel Run or "chase" version was 200. The Rebel Run issue is changed to black paint with blue metalflake, along with electric blue lightning bolts.	1,300 200	22.00 93.00
2009 / Super Flames 2	**Burnout Bus**. Issued in January, 2009. Green and black body with flame deco. Regular run was 1,300, while the Rebel Run or "chase" version was 200. The Rebel Run issue is changed to metallic blue and black.	1,300 200	20.00 99.00

Year / Model	Description	Run #	Value
2009 / High Roller	Issued in February, 2009. Matte black paint scheme with Las Vegas and casino graphics. Regular run was 1,300, while the Rebel Run or "chase" version was 200. The Rebel Run issue is changed to a red roof, with the same graphics.	1,300 200	27.00 65.00
2009 / Hot Wheels Nationals (Reston, VA)	Issued in March, 2009 in commemoration of the 9th Annual Hot Wheels Collectors Nationals. Red, white and blue paint scheme with iconic Washington D.C. graphics. Regular run was 1,300, while the Rebel Run or "chase" version was 400. The Rebel Run issue has the same graphics, but also has a tiny imprint of Abraham Lincoln and 1809-2009 on the rear of the bus.	1,300 400	28.00 43.00
2009 / Surfin' Series 7	**Cal Woodie**. Issued in June, 2009. Green with faux woodgrain on the sides, and two surfboards on the roof. Regular run was 1,300, while the Rebel Run or "chase" version was 200. The Rebel Run issue has pearl white paint, with two surfboards on the roof, with the same deco.	1,300 200	29.00 70.00
2009 / Surfin' Series 8	**Waikiki Wagon**. Issued in June, 2009. Orange, with hula dancer on the roof, and surfboards mounted to the sides. Regular run was 1,300, while the Rebel Run or "chase" version was 200. The Rebel Run issue has lavender paint with two surfboards on the sides, and the same deco.	1,300 200	30.00 81.00

Year / Model	Description	Run #	Value
2009 / Bomber Drag Bus	**Happy Hour.** Issued in July, 2009. Steel-grey paint with redhead and brunette dancers on the roof. Regular run was 1,300, while the Rebel Run or "chase" version was 200. The Rebel Run issue has the same deco, but the redhead has been changed to a blonde dancer, and there is a "Kilroy" tampo on the side.	1,300 200	23.00 55.00
2009 / Summer Smash 2	Issued in August, 2009. Metallic teal paint with flames and Summer Smash 2 deco. Regular run was 1,250, while the Attendee issue was limited to 450. The Rebel Run or "chase" version was 250. The Attendee issue came in black, with the same deco, and the Rebel Run issue came in dark-blue paint, with the same deco.	1,250 450 250	31.00 40.00 46.00
2009 / Halloween	**Werewolf.** Issued in October, 2009. Black, with yellow werewolf deco and yellow "wolf eyes" for headlights. Regular run was 1,300, while the Rebel Run or "chase" version was 200. The Rebel Run issue has the same deco, but with blue werewolf deco and "wolf eyes."	1,300 200	34.00 90.00
2009 / Outlaw Bus	Issued in November, 2009. Burnt red, with a brown roof and "outlaw" wanted posters of the "Diecast Desperado" and "Blisterpack Jack." Regular run was 1,000, the Rebel Run or "chase" version was 300, and the Titanus run was 200. The Rebel Run issue has the same deco, but with wanted posters of "The Cut-Throat Barber" and "Lethal Souza." The Titanus run featured a silver bison coin on the roof.	1,000 300 200	23.00 59.00 86.00

Year / Model	Description	Run #	Value
2009 / Winter Wagon	**Snow Drift**. Issued in December, 2009. Metallic red/white with "Winter Wagon"/flame deco and green windows. Regular run was 1,300, while the Rebel Run or "chase" version was 200. The Rebel Run issue metallic green paint with red windows and the same deco.	1,300 200	27.00 102.00
2010 / Gear Head	Issued in January, 2010. Copper-plated body, with "Gear Head"/gear deco. Regular run was 1,300, while the Rebel Run or "chase" version was 200. The Rebel Run issue is gold, with the same deco.	1,300 200	29.00 88.00
2010 / Diecast Super Convention	Platinum Edition. Issued in March, 2010 to commemorate the Diecast Super Convention. Black fade to silver, with flames and DSC deco. Regular run was 1,000, while the Rebel Run or "chase" version was 250. The Rebel Run issue is silver fade to black, with the same deco.	1,000 250	25.00 65.00
2010 / St. Louis Nationals	Issued in April, 2010, in commemoration of the 10th Hot Wheels Collectors Nationals. Black, with steamboat and archway deco. Regular run was 1,300, while the Rebel Run or "chase" version was 400. The Rebel Run issue is the same color and deco, but has a hidden image of Mark Twain in the steam.	1,300 400	31.00 61.00

Year / Model	Description	Run #	Value
2010 / Magical Weekend of Cars	Issued in June, 2010, in commemoration of the 1st Magical Weekend of Cars in Orlando, FL. Purple/white, with "2010 Magical Weekend" deco. Regular run was 1,200, the Rebel Run or "chase" version was 250, and the Charity Run was 250. The Rebel Run issue is blue/white, with the same deco, and the Charity Run is green/white, with the same deco.	1,200 250 RR 250 CH	26.00 61.00 56.00
2010 / Aqua-Haulic	Issued in July, 2010. Aqua paint with stripe/"Aqua-Haulic" deco. Regular run was 1,300, while the Rebel Run or "chase" version was 200. The Rebel Run (Choco-Haulic) issue is brown with stripe/"Choco-Haulic" deco.	1,300 200	25.00 58.00
2010 / Summer Smash 3	Issued in August, 2010, in commemoration of Summer Smash 3, held in Warwick, Rhode Island. White/orange, with two surfboards mounted on the roof. Regular run was 1,250, the Rebel Run or "chase" version was 250, and the Attendee version was 500. The Rebel Run issue is "Bonzer Blue," with the same deco, and the Attendee version is "Offshore Orange," with the same deco.	1,200 500 250	31.00 36.00 64.00
2010 / Canada Convention	Issued in September, 2010, in commemoration of the 1st Canada Diecast Convention in Niagara Falls, ON. White body with maple leaf deco. Regular run was 1,250, while the Rebel Run or "chase" version was 250. The Rebel Run issue is black, with the same deco.	1,250 250	25.00 95.00

Year / Model	Description	Run #	Value
2010 / Halloween	**Ghost Flames**. Issued in October, 2010. Black chrome body with "ghost flames." Regular run was 1,300, while the Rebel Run or "chase" version was 200. The Rebel Run issue is silver chrome, with the same deco.	1,300 200	37.00 67.00
2010 / USA Eagle Bus	Issued in November, 2010. Blue/white body with "USA"/eagle deco. Regular run was 1,300, while the Rebel Run or "chase" version was 200. The Rebel Run issue is chrome blue/white, with the same deco.	1,300 200	25.00 95.00
2010 / Winter Wagon	**Icicle**. Issued in December, 2010. Blue body with "Winter Wagon"/icicle deco. Regular run was 1,300, while the Rebel Run or "chase" version was 200. The Rebel Run issue is white, with the same deco.	1,300 200	23.00 56.00
2011 / Loyalty Rewards Bus	Issued in March, 2011. Black body with "Liberty Legion" deco and "Liberty Loyalist" stamp. Liberty Loyalist stamp run was 604, while the Liberty Loyalist 100% version was 528.	604 528	26.00 29.00

Year / Model	Description	Run #	Value
2011 / Freaky Tiki 2	Issued in March, 2011. Flat-black body with orange, red, and green pinstriping. Regular run was 800, while the Rebel Run or "chase" version was 200. The Rebel Run issue is also black, but with fuchsia, blue, and green pinstriping. The option of a blue surfboard was available on both models.	800 200	29.00 63.00
2011 / Surfin' Freaky Tiki 2	Issued in March, 2011. Flat-black body with orange, red, and green pinstriping, with a red board. Regular run was 800, while the Rebel Run or "chase" version was 200. The Rebel Run issue is also black, but with fuchsia, blue, and green pinstriping, with a blue board.	800 200	30.00 73.00
2011 / Cincinnati Nationals	Issued in March, 2011, commemorating the Hot Wheels Collectors Nationals Convention in Cincinnati, OH. "5-Alarm Red" body with "Welcome Collectors"/pig/beer deco. Regular run was 1,000, while the Rebel Run or "chase" version was 200. The Rebel Run issue is "Charred Black," with the same deco.	1,000 200	27.00 49.00
2011 / Diecast Hall of Fame	Issued in May, 2011, commemorating the Diecast Hall of Fame. Pewter, with black roof and "DHOF" deco. Regular run was 1,250, the Rebel Run or "chase" version was 250, and the Dinner version was 250. The Rebel Run issue is aluminum/black with the same deco, and the Dinner version is metallic red/black with the same deco.	1,250 250 RR 250 D	28.00 65.00 69.00

Year / Model	Description	Run #	Value
2011 / Nashville Collector's Experience	**Music City Splitty**. Issued in June, 2011, commemorating the 2011 Collector's Experience that took place in Nashville, Tennessee. "Black gold" with "Collector Experience"/guitar deco. Regular run was 1,250, the Rebel Run or "chase" version was 250, and the Dinner version was 250. The Rebel Run issue is "Dark Sapphire" with the same deco, and the Dinner version is "White Diamond" with the same deco.	1,250 250 RR 250 D	31.00 65.00 71.00
2011 / Kruizinwagon	**K2 Red**. Issued in July, 2011. Flat-burnt red body with "Kruizinwagon"/flame deco. Regular run was 900, while the Rebel Run or "chase" version was 100. The Rebel Run issue has the same deco, but also has an extra kangaroo tampo on the rear quarter panel. NOTE: Approximately 10% have a rosy shade of red versus the normal faded red.	900 100	27.00 125.00
2011 / Kruizinwagon	**K2 Yellow**. Issued in July, 2011. Flat-yellow body with "Kruizinwagon"/flame deco. Regular run was 900, while the Rebel Run or "chase" version was 100. The Rebel Run issue has the same deco, but also has an extra kangaroo tampo on the rear quarter panel.	900 100	25.00 118.00
2011 / Summer Smash 4	Issued in September, 2011. Antifreeze body with "Summer Smash"/Splittin' Image/Boneshaker deco. Regular run was 1,250, while the Rebel Run or "chase" version was 250. The Attendee issue run was 500. The Rebel Run issue is Rose Pink, and has the same deco, while the Attendee version is blue, with the same deco.	1,250 500 250	32.00 61.00 104.00

Year / Model	Description	Run #	Value
2011 / Halloween	**Gone Surfin'**. Issued in October, 2011. Purple/green/black body with "Gone Surfin"/fish skeleton deco, and a black surfboard on the roof. Regular run was 1,300, while the Rebel Run or "chase" version was 200. The Rebel Run issue is Green/purple/black, with the same deco.	1,300 200	28.00 61.00
2011 / Rhode Island Hot Wheels Club	Issued in November, 2011. White/blue body with "RIHWC"/wave deco. Regular run was 1,000, while the Rebel Run or "chase" version was 200. The Rebel Run issue is grey/blue, with the same deco.	1,000 200	22.00 56.00
2011 / Kruizinwagon	**K2 Black**. Issued in December, 2011. Flat-black body with "Kruizinwagon"/flame deco. Regular run was 900, while the Rebel Run or "chase" version was 100. The Rebel Run issue has the same deco, but also has an extra kangaroo tampo on the rear quarter panel.	900 100	23.00 122.00
2012 / Superflames 3	**Hot Stuff**. Issued in January, 2012. Yellow/black body with flame deco. Regular run was 1,000, while the Rebel Run or "chase" version was 200. The Rebel Run issue has is hot pink/black, with the same deco.	1,000 200	31.00 92.00

Year / Model	Description	Run #	Value
2012 / Hot Streak	Issued in February, 2012, commemorating the 2012 Diecast Super Convention in Las Vegas, Nevada. White body with playing card/flame deco. Regular run was 1,000, the Rebel Run or "chase" version was 250, and the Dinner version was 250. The Rebel Run issue is black, with the same deco, and the Dinner version is yellow, with the same deco.	1,000 250 RR 250 D	27.00 61.00 76.00
2012 / Van-Go!	Issued in March, 2012. "Burnout Black"/white body with "Van-Go"/checkerboard deco. Regular run was 1,000, while the Rebel Run or "chase" version was 200. The Rebel Run issue is "Racing Red"/white, with the same deco.	1,000 200	26.00 64.00
2012 / Civil War	**Confederate**. Issued in June, 2012. Grey/red body with "Our Dixie Forever" deco. Regular run was 1,000, while the Rebel Run or "chase" version was 200. The Rebel Run issue is the same color, but has a General Lee tampo on the rear panel.	1,000 200	28.00 79.00
2012 / Civil War	**Union**. Issued in June, 2012. Blue/red body with "Rally 'Round the Flag, Boys!" deco. Regular run was 1,000, while the Rebel Run or "chase" version was 200. The Rebel Run issue is the same color, but has a General Grant tampo on the rear.	1,000 200	27.00 81.00

Year / Model	Description	Run #	Value
2012 / Summer Smash 5	Issued in August, 2012 in commemoration of Summer Smash 5, held in Warwick, Rhode Island. "Scorched Black" body with flame deco. Regular run was 1,000, while the Rebel Run or "chase" version was 200. The Rebel Run issue is also black, but with a red roof and the same deco.	1,000 200	27.00 45.00
2012 / Halloween	**Black Widow**. Issued in October, 2012. Matte-black body with "Happy Halloween!"/black widow deco. Regular run was 1,000, while the Rebel Run or "chase" version was 200. The Rebel Run issue is cobalt blue, with additional fly deco on the side rear panel.	1,000 200	26.00 79.00
2012 / Christmas	**Mad Dasher**. Issued in December, 2012. Red/green/silver body with snow spray and "Mad Dasher" deco. Regular run was 1,000, while the Rebel Run or "chase" version was 200. The Rebel Run issue is white/green/silver.	1,000 200	27.00 103.00
2013 / Indianapolis Nationals	Issued in April, 2013, in commemoration of the Hot Wheels Collectors Nationals in Indianapolis. Red/black body with "Indianapolis"/car deco. Regular run was 1,000, while the Rebel Run or "chase" version was 200. The Rebel Run issue is gold/black, with the same deco.	1,000 200	33.00 65.00

Year / Model	Description	Run #	Value
2013 – Independence Day	**Fireworks**. Issued in July, 2013. Red/black body with "Independence Day"/fireworks/blue flame deco. Regular run was 1,000, while the Rebel Run or "chase" version was 200. The Rebel Run issue is the same color, but with purple deco.	1,000 200	34.00 60.00
2013 / Brazil Convention	**Wild Wing**. Issued in August, 2013. White/green body with pinstriping deco and a white surfboard. Regular run was 1,300, while the Rebel Run or "chase" version was 200. The Rebel Run issue is glossy black, with a black surfboard and the same deco.	1,300 200	31.00 117.00
2013 / Malibu Bus	Issued in October, 2013. Cherry-red body with woodgrain roof, "Malibu" deco and two surfboards. Regular run was 1,000, while the Rebel Run or "chase" version was 200. Rebel Run issue #1 is "Mali-blue" with the same deco, and the convention version is "Seafoam Green," with the same deco.	1,000 200 RR 200 C	31.00 66.00 62.00
2013 / Christmas	**Santa's Sled**. Issued in December, 2014. Metallic green/red body with "Santa's Sled"/holiday deco. Regular run was 1,000, while the Rebel Run or "chase" version was 200. The Rebel Run issue is white/red, with the same deco.	1,000 200	32.00 61.00

Year / Model	Description	Run #	Value
2014 / Chicago Nationals	Issued in April, 2014. "Saucy Red" body with "Chicago Collectors"/pizza deco. Regular run was 1,000, the Rebel Run or "chase" version was 200, and the convention edition was 200. The Rebel Run issue is the same color, but with "Rebel Run" on the wing, and mushrooms added to the roof. The convention edition is "Greasy Orange," with the same deco as the Regular run.	1,000 200 RR 200 CN	25.00 84.00 31.00
2014 / Halloween	**Butcher Bus**. Issued in October, 2014. Black body with blue eyes for headlights and 6-Spoke Pro Circuit wheels. Regular run was 1,000, while the Rebel Run or "chase" version was 200. The Rebel Run issue is also black, but with green eyes and maggots.	1,000 200	33.00 98.00
2015 / Moonshine Bus	Issued in July, 2015. Copper-plated body with Star Pro Circuit wheels. Regular run was 1,000, while the Rebel Run or "chase" version was 200. The Rebel Run issue is brass-plated, and has the same graphics as the Regular version.	1,000 200	NEW NEW
2015 / Bootlegger Bus	Issued in July, 2015. Matte-black body with black 5-Spoke wheels. Regular run was 1,000, while the Rebel Run or "chase" version was 200. The Rebel Run issue is matte-chrome, and has the same graphics as the Regular version.	1,000 200	NEW NEW

Year / Model	Description	Run #	Value
2015 / Flamethrower Bus	Issued in September, 2015 in commemoration of the Brazil Colecon convention. Black/green body with Pro Circuit wheels. Regular run was 1,000, while the Rebel Run or "chase" version was 200. The Rebel Run issue has a black body, and there is also a Convention issue with a black/yellow body and white roof.	1,000 200 RR 200 C	NEW NEW NEW
2015 / Halloween	**Day of The Dead**. Issued in October, 2015. "Glowing" teal and glossy black body with black chassis and black 5-Spoke wheels. Regular run was 1,000, while the Rebel Run or "chase" version was 200. The Rebel Run issue is "Glowing" purple and black, and has the same graphics as the Regular version.	1,000 200	NEW NEW

Charity / Misc LP Issues

This section will cover all charity and convention Liberty Promotions issues that weren't listed in the regular guide. Unfortunately, due to the limited nature of these buses, there will be quite a few "NRS" annotations (No Recent Sales). These will be updated for the next volume.

Year / Model	Description	Run #	Value
2008 / Chicago Nationals (Charity)	**Children's Miracle Network.** Issued in April, 2008. White/red bus with Nationals logo on roof, checkered flames, CMN logo on sides and Star Pro Circuit hubs with Goodyear tires. Limited to a run of 225.	225	110.00
2008 / Chicago Nationals (Charity)	**Children's Miracle Network.** Issued in April, 2008. Black/red bus with Nationals logo on roof, checkered flames, CMN logo on sides and Star Pro Circuit hubs with Goodyear tires. Limited to a run of 225	75	NRS
2008 / Tattoo Bus	**Liberty Legionnaire.** Issued in June, 2008. Tan body with eagle/tribal deco on the sides. Available in 4 variations: Discoverus (ltd. 600), Commendus, (ltd. 600), Prominus (ltd. 500) and Titanus (ltd. 100)/	600 (D) 600 (C) 500 (P) 100 (T)	38.00 17.00 28.00 397.00

Year / Model	Description	Run #	Value
2008 / Summer Smash 1 (Charity)	**Make a Wish**. Issued in August, 2008 as a charity edition for Summer Smash held in Warwick, Rhode Island. White/red body with stripe deco, Summer Smash logo on roof and Make a Wish logo on wing. 6-Spoke Pro Circuits, with GoodYear tires.	250	39.00
2008 / HW's 40th Ann. (Charity)	**Make a Wish**. Issued in October, 2008 for the 22nd Annual Collector's Convention. White/silver body with 40th logo on the roof and Make a Wish logo on the wing. Star Pro Circuit hubs with Goodyear tires. Limited to a run of 225.	225	NRS
2008 / HW's 40th Ann. (Charity)	**Make a Wish**. Issued in October, 2008 for the 22nd Annual Collector's Convention. Gold/black body with 40th logo on the roof and Make a Wish logo on the wing. Star Pro Circuit hubs with Goodyear tires. Limited to a run of 100.	100	NRS
2008 / HW's 40th Ann. (Charity)	**Make a Wish**. Issued in October, 2008 for the 22nd Annual Collector's Convention. Blue/white body with 40th logo on the roof and Make a Wish logo on the wing. Star Pro Circuit hubs with Goodyear tires. Limited to a run of 75.	75	NRS

Year / Model	Description	Run #	Value
2009 / 9th Nationals (Charity)	**Children's Miracle Network.** Issued in March, 2009 as a charity edition for the 9th Annual Collector's Nationals held in Reston, Virginia. Pink body with stripe deco, Nationals logo on roof and Children's Miracle Network logo on rear quarter panel. Star Pro Circuits, with GoodYear tires.	250	NRS
2009 / 9th Nationals (Charity)	**Children's Miracle Network.** Issued in March, 2009 for the 9th Annual Collector's Nationals held in Reston, Virginia. Silver body with stripe deco, Nationals logo on roof and Children's Miracle Network logo on rear quarter panel. . Star Pro Circuit hubs with Goodyear tires. Limited to a run of 100.	100	NRS
2009 / 9th Nationals (Charity)	**Children's Miracle Network.** Issued in March, 2009 for the 9th Annual Collector's Nationals held in Reston, Virginia. Yellow body with stripe deco, Nationals logo on roof and Children's Miracle Network logo on rear quarter panel. Star Pro Circuit hubs with Goodyear tires. Limited to a run of 75.	75	NRS
2009 / Summer Smash 2 (Charity)	**Make a Wish.** Issued in August, 2009 for the 2nd Summer Smash held in Warwick, Rhode Island. Blue/white body with Summer Smash logo on the roof, and Make a Wish logo on the wing. Star Pro Circuit hubs with Goodyear tires. Limited to a run of 175.	175	47.00

Year / Model	Description	Run #	Value
2009 / Summer Smash 2 (Charity)	**Make a Wish**. Issued in August, 2009 for the 2nd Summer Smash held in Warwick, Rhode Island. Gold/black body with Summer Smash logo on the roof, and Make a Wish logo on the wing. Star Pro Circuit hubs with Goodyear tires. Limited to a run of 150.	150	60.00
2009 / 23rd Convention (Charity)	**Make a Wish**. Issued in September, 2009 for the 23rd Annual Collector's Convention. Gold/black body with Convention logo on roof and Make a Wish logo on the wing. Star Pro Circuit hubs with Goodyear tires. Limited to a run of 250.	250	NRS
2009 / 23rd Convention (Charity)	**Make a Wish**. Issued in September, 2009 for the 23rd Annual Collector's Convention. Silver/black body with Convention logo on roof and Make a Wish logo on the wing. Star Pro Circuit hubs with Goodyear tires. Limited to a run of 100.	100	NRS
2009 / 23rd Convention (Charity)	**Make a Wish**. Issued in September, 2009 for the 23rd Annual Collector's Convention. Pink/black body with Convention logo on roof and Make a Wish logo on the wing. Star Pro Circuit hubs with Goodyear tires. Limited to a run of 75.	75	NRS

Year / Model	Description	Run #	Value
2010 / Diecast Super Convention	Issued in February, 2010 for the Diecast Super Convention held in Las Vegas, Nevada. Blue/white body with DSC logo on the roof, and flames. Star Pro Circuit hubs with Goodyear tires. Limited to a run of 1,000.	1,000	34.00
2010 / Diecast Super Convention	Issued in February, 2010 for the Diecast Super Convention held in Las Vegas, Nevada. Purple/black body with DSC logo on the roof, and flames. Star Pro Circuit hubs with Goodyear tires. Limited to a run of 250.	250	42.00
2010 / Diecast Super Convention	Issued in February, 2010 for the Diecast Super Convention held in Las Vegas, Nevada. Pink body with DSC logo on the roof, and flames. Star Pro Circuit hubs with Goodyear tires. Limited to a run of 250.	250	58.00
2010 / Magical Weekend (Charity)	**Make a Wish**. Issued in June, 2010 for the Magical Weekend of Cars. Green/white body with Magical Convention logo on the roof. 6-Spoke Pro Circuit hubs with Goodyear tires. Limited to a run of 250.	250	60.00

Year / Model	Description	Run #	Value
2010 / Summer Smash 3 (Charity)	Issued in August, 2010 for Summer Smash 3, held in Warwick, Rhode Island. Blue/white body with Summer Smash logo on the roof, and "This Way To The Hot Wheels" deco on the sides. Star Pro Circuit hubs with Goodyear tires. Limited to a run of 150.	150	55.00
2010 / Summer Smash 3 (Charity)	Issued in August, 2010 for Summer Smash 3, held in Warwick, Rhode Island. Orange/white body with Summer Smash logo on the roof, and "This Way To The Hot Wheels" deco on the sides. Star Pro Circuit hubs with Goodyear tires. Limited to a run of 150.	150	55.00
2011 / Diecast Hall of Fame (Charity)	Issued in May, 2011 for the Diecast Hall of Fame in Las Vegas, Nevada. Candy red body with HOF logo on the roof. 6-Spoke Pro Circuit hubs with Goodyear tires. Limited to a run of 250.	250	61.00
2011 / Collector's Experience (Charity)	Issued in June, 2011 for the Collector's Experience. White Diamond body with Collector's Experience logo on the roof. 6-Spoke Pro Circuit hubs with Goodyear tires. Limited to a run of 250.	250	NRS

Year / Model	Description	Run #	Value
2011 / Summer Smash 4 (Charity)	Issued in August, 2011 for Summer Smash 4, held in Warwick, Rhode Island. Red body with Summer Smash logo on the roof, and sun deco on the sides. 6-Spoke Pro Circuit hubs with Goodyear tires. Limited to a run of 150.	150	67.00
2011 / Summer Smash 4 (Charity)	Issued in August, 2011 for Summer Smash 4, held in Warwick, Rhode Island. Black body with Summer Smash logo on the roof, and sun deco on the sides. 6-Spoke Pro Circuit hubs with Goodyear tires. Limited to a run of 150.	150	69.00
2012 / Summer Smash 5	**Attendee Version.** Issued in August, 2012 for Summer Smash 5, held in Warwick Rhode Island. Ripe Peach body with white wing, stripe deco and white surfboards. 6-Spoke Pro Circuit hubs with Goodyear tires. Limited to a run of 400.	400	50.00
2012 / Summer Smash 5	**Dinner Version.** Issued in August, 2012 for Summer Smash 5, held in Warwick Rhode Island. Sunset Pink body with white wing, stripe deco and white surfboards. 6-Spoke Pro Circuit hubs with Goodyear tires. Limited to a run of 300.	300	NRS

Year / Model	Description	Run #	Value
 2012 / Summer Smash 5	**Breakfast Version**. Issued in August, 2012 for Summer Smash 5, held in Warwick Rhode Island. Mint Green body with white wing, stripe deco and white surfboards. 6-Spoke Pro Circuit hubs with Goodyear tires. Limited to a run of 200.	200	NRS
 2015 / Colecon Brazil	Issued in July, 2015 in commemoration of the Colecon convention in Brazil. Black/yellow body with white roof, Colecon 2015 graphics and Star Pro Circuit wheels. Limited to a run of 200.	200	NEW

A little nostalgia never hurts…

Gallery

This gallery will showcase most of the highly-collectible Rebel Run issues issued by Liberty Promotions. Values for each can be found in the Liberty section of the guide. A couple of Limited Attendee and Charity models are included here as well.

2004 Sturgis Set (Gal) Ltd. to 200

2004 Drag-On Wagon – Ltd. to 200

2004 Drag-On Wagon – Ltd. to 200

2005 Collection Builder – Ltd. to 200

2005 Collection Builder – Ltd. to 200

2005 Pirates 1 (Scourge of the Sea) – Ltd. to 200

2005 Pirates 1 (Treasure) – Ltd. to 200

2005 Sturgis (Gal) – Ltd. to 200

2005 Sturgis (Guy) – Ltd. to 200

2005 Halloween (Dungeon) – Ltd. to 200

2005 Halloween (Witch) – Ltd. to 200

2005 Surfin' Series 1 (Woodie) – Ltd. to 200

2005 Surfin' Series 2 (Wave Rider) – Ltd. to 200

2006 Cops & Robbers (Cops) – Ltd. to 200

2006 Cops & Robbers (Robbers) – Ltd. to 200

2006 Pirates 2 (Capt. Kidd/Silver) – Ltd. to 150

2006 Pirates 2 (Capt. Kidd/Gold) – Ltd. to 50

2006 Pirates 2 (Blackbeard/Silver) – Ltd. to 150

2006 Pirates 2 (Blackbeard/Gold) – Ltd. to 50

2006 Fire & Ice (Ice) – Ltd. to 200

2006 Fire & Ice (Fire) – Ltd. to 200

2006 Halloween (Vampire) – Ltd. to 200

2006 Halloween (Frankenstein) – Ltd. to 200

2006 Bomber Bus (Yankee Gal) – Ltd. to 200

2006 Fighter Bus (Flying Tiger) – Ltd. to 200

2007 Alien (Abduction) – Ltd. to 300

2007 Alien (Abduction) – Ltd. to 200

2007 Alien (Autopsy) – Ltd. to 300

2007 Alien (Autopsy) – Ltd. to 200

2007 Surfin' Series 3 (Fire Woodie) – Ltd. to 200

2007 Surfin' Series 4 (Freaky Tiki) – Ltd. to 200

2007 Pirates 3 (Mutineer/Silver) – Ltd. to 150

2007 Pirates 3 (Mutineer/Gold) – Ltd. to 50

2007 Pirates 3 (Sneak/Silver) – Ltd. to 150

2007 Pirates 3 (Mutineer/Gold) – Ltd. to 50

2008 Surfin' Series 5 (Bamboozled) – Ltd. to 200

2008 Surfin' Series 6 (Shark Attack) – Ltd. to 200

2008 Superflames 1 (Blazin' Bus) – Ltd. to 200

2008 Summer Smash 1 (Rebel Run) – Ltd. to 200

2008 Summer Smash 1 (Attendee) – Ltd. to 250

2008 Halloween (Zombie Outbreak) – Ltd. to 50

2008 Route 66 – Ltd. to 200

2008 LightningWagon – Ltd. to 200

2008 Superflames 2 (Burnout Bus) – Ltd. to 200

2009 High Roller – Ltd. to 200

2009 Surfin' Series 7 (Cal Woodie) – Ltd. to 200

2009 Surfin' Series 8 (Waikiki Wagon) – Ltd. to 200

2009 Bomber Bus (Happy Hour) – Ltd. to 200

2009 Summer Smash 2 (Rebel Run) – Ltd. to 250

2009 Summer Smash 2 (Attendee) – Ltd. to 250

2009 Halloween (Werewolf) – Ltd. to 200

2009 Christmas (Winter Wagon) – Ltd. to 200

2010 Gear Head – Ltd. to 200

2010 Diecast Super Convention – Ltd. to 250

2010 Magical Weekend (Rebel Run) – Ltd. to 250

2010 Magical Weekend (Charity) – Ltd. to 250

2010 Choco-Haulic – Ltd. to 200

2010 Summer Smash 3 (R/Run) – Ltd. to 250

2010 Summer Smash 3 (Att.) – Ltd. to 500

2010 Diecast Super Convention – Ltd. to 250

2010 USA Eagle – Ltd. to 200

2010 Winter Wagon (Icycle) – Ltd. to 200

2011 Liberty Loyalist – Ltd. to 528

2011 Freaky Tiki 2 – Ltd. to 200

2011 Freaky Tiki 2 – Ltd. to 200

2011 Cincinnati Nationals – Ltd. to 200

2011 Diecast Hall of Fame – Ltd. to 250

2011 Summer Smash 4 – Ltd. to 250

2011 Summer Smash 4 (Att) – Ltd. to 500

2011 RI Hot Wheels Club – Ltd. to 200

2011 Halloween – Ltd. to 200

2011 Superflames 3 – Ltd. to 200

2012 Hot Streak – Ltd. to 250

2012 Hot Streak (Att) – Ltd. to 250

2012 Van-Go! – Ltd. to 200

2012 Summer Smash 5 – Ltd. to 200

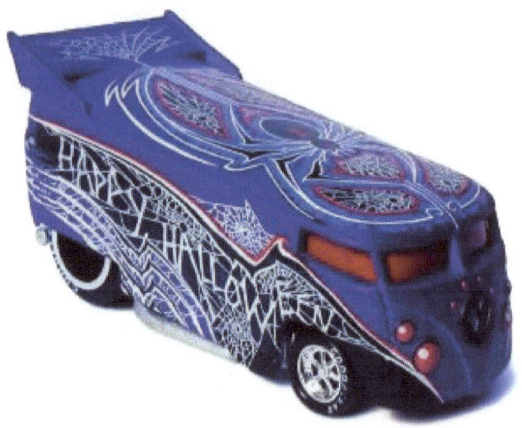 

2012 Halloween – Ltd. to 200   2012 Christmas – Ltd. to 200

2013 Indianapolis Nationals – Ltd. to 200   2013 Independence Day – Ltd. to 200

2013 Brazil Wild Wing – Ltd. to 200   2013 Surfin' Series 12 (Malibu) – Ltd. to 200

2013 Surfin' Series 12 (Att) – Ltd. to 200

2013 Christmas – Ltd. to 200

2014 Chicago Nationals (Conv) – Ltd. to 200

2014 Halloween – Ltd. to 200

2015 Moonshine Bus – Ltd. to 200

2015 Bootlegger Bus – Ltd. to 200

2015 Flamethrower Bus – Ltd. to 200   2015 Halloween – Ltd. to 200

Interview With Lee Pearlman, Creative Director at Liberty Promotions

What influenced you to start making your own diecast promotions?
Well, I've always been a car guy. Since I was a kid, I was fascinated with cars. My parents didn't have anything great, like muscle cars, but I did like some of the cars we had. There was a '68 Cutlass and a '69 Eldorado that I have fond memories of. We even had the "Chevy Chase" green '71 Country Squire station wagon that I traveled in, coast-to-coast round-trip, in 1974. I sat or slept in the very back with my sister, without a seatbelt, of course, the whole way from Washington, DC to San Diego, and back again. I loved the cars some of the teenagers drove in the neighborhood. I can remember a Super Bee and a '67 Camaro with Cragar mags. I just loved the way those wheels reflected the sun.

My favorite toys were Hot Wheels, without a doubt. I never liked GI Joes, or many of the things other kids played with. When I wasn't racing them down tracks, I built little cities and roads for them and just let my imagination go. I really liked the prototype cars, like the Mod Quad, Mutt Mobile, S'Cool Bus, and Splittin' Image. The Splittin' Image is still my favorite Hot Wheels car. Nothing wrong with the Chargers and Mustangs, but I didn't think they were as cool. It seems like I only took a break from playing with the cars whenever an episode of Speed Racer was on.

Once it came time for me to own a car, I bought a '69 442. I owned several different 442s and Cutlasses for many years. I also had an AMX. It wasn't always easy owning those cars without a garage or the best of tools to work on them with. None of them were cherry. I continued to buy an occasional die-cast car into adulthood, but only sparingly. I just picked up the occasional model of a real car that I admired. I was unaware that there were a lot of adult collectors out there until 1995, after I started seeing more and more other people looking at the cars in the toy aisles. Finally, I went to my first toy show in early 1996 and was amazed. I started buying a lot more cars after that!

During most of my 20s, I had worked with computers doing programming. I enjoyed some of the challenges, but I could also get bored with it. So, I took a job in advertising with a company that specialized in automotive advertising. This enabled me to hang out in shops and be around cars more. I didn't want to be a mechanic, but I wanted to be around people and cars. After about a year with that company, I decided to start my own company doing the same thing. I worked with various franchisees of well-known service centers, like Goodyear, Jiffy Lube, etc. I had a particularly good relationship with a chain of stores called All Tune & Lube, especially in the Southwest region. (I live in Dallas.) One day it occurred to me that it would be a really good idea to do a promotional Hot Wheels car for automotive service centers. Big cars and little cars go together, I figured. It was good exposure for the Hot Wheels brand, and it was good promotion for the auto centers. So, we did our first die-cast car for All Tune & Lube in 1997, which was a black VW bus with flames. It caused quite a stir. I moved on to doing cars for Jiffy Lube and Penske Auto Centers, as many people know. That was many years ago, and things have definitely evolved. We're more collector-oriented now, but we still do many corporate/promo cars.

Are you a collector, yourself? What are your interests?
I am definitely a collector. It's a lot of fun. I have to contain myself, though. It can get out of hand quickly, as you all know. My other interests include attending real car shows and events. I spend a lot of time with my son, who also loves cars. Otherwise, I like to play basketball to have fun and keep in shape (about three times a week), even though I'm not very tall.

Liberty makes a lot of VW Drag Buses; where do you get your castings?
We've have had a very good relationship with Mattel for many years and were afforded the opportunity to buy many of them a while back. In some cases, we got to purchase entire runs with crooked logos or other errors, but we were required to strip them down and not release them with the mistakes on them. We've purchased over 375,000 buses directly from Mattel. These include promotional models for All Tune & Lube, Penske, Jiffy Lube, some "mistake" models and some CD-ROM packaged buses which were liquidated to us by Mattel. In the case of Penske Auto Centers, they closed their operations before they had an opportunity to use two of the three versions produced. We acquired these unused pieces at that time. Additionally, we've purchased overstock from other sources, leftover quantities from various runs, such as the Military and VW Club releases, as well as more of the CD-ROM buses. We have plenty of pieces to make our very limited, high-quality custom runs for the next several years.

How do you come up with the deco/designs for your VW Bus issues?
That's my main job, you could say, other than managing the day-to-day operations. I do get some help with this from the artists that we use and also collectors. Otherwise, I just look for inspiration in my travels, other aspects of life, and hanging out at car events. I'm not really that good at drawing. I can do it a little bit, but it's a chore. A capable artist is typically much faster and more fluid than I am, I guess because it doesn't really come all that naturally to me. I have plenty of pictures in my head, but it's hard to put them down. I work with people that seem to read my mind really well and execute the ideas better than I could. Without trying to sound like I'm patting myself on my back, I think my best attribute in this regard is that I know cool when I see it.

What process do you utilize for deco application on the Buses?
With very rare exception, we use tampo (pad) printing. This, of course, is the traditional way of printing on cars going back to about 1974. There are newer methods involving decals and direct inkjet, but they don't have the same clarity and pop that tampo printing does. You can see the "pixels" with the other methods. These other methods get better all the time, but we plan to stick with the tampo printing, if for no other reason than for the tradition. Of course, it's the most expensive way to do the deco, which is why you see companies going for the alternatives. I think discerning collectors appreciate the look and feel of good quality tampo printing.

The values for Liberty Buses seem to hold very well. What does this suggest to you about the quality of the Buses?
I think it's a combination of things –quality of the paint and deco, creative and thoughtful artwork, integrity of Liberty Promotions, good customer service, etc. All of these things contribute to the collectability. We try really hard to make something cool and desirable, and we appreciate any and all feedback.

What was the inspiration behind adding the successful "Rebel Run" concept to the regular lines?
It just kind of started with the first run we did where we were completely responsible for the paint and deco, which was the Kruizinwagon bus. There's a very cool company in Australia that customizes and restores VW buses, which was the inspiration for the deco on that one. Anyway, I just had a thought that was something along the lines of, "Wouldn't it be a hoot if we put a little kangaroo on a small percentage of them in order to make an uncommon variation?" I thought it might make people a little bit excited or a little bit crazy, one or the other; but I didn't think that it would be such a big deal. Of course, then we had to come up with a name and a logo for the variation, because we knew that collectors were going to demand that every run have a Rebel Run.

What influenced your decision to utilize acrylic cases versus blister cards for the VW Bus line?
Well, I'm a purist. I also don't like clutter, even though my desk is cluttered. I like having cars loose, so that I can touch them and clearly see them. Sometimes people get more concerned about the packaging than the car itself. I want collectors to be able to take their cars out of the packaging without feeling like they're devaluing them, or even if they don't then at least they can see them clearly through the hard clear acrylic. I am pretty sure that our buses would be more popular in blister. I've definitely thought about offering them both ways –in blister and in acrylic cases. I have to say, though, that I'm really glad to not have to deal with complaints about imperfect packaging. This used to be a nightmare. A few collectors have told me that they don't even open the boxes of the cars they get from us. That makes me cringe.

Is the VW Bus casting one that you personally collect?
Absolutely! I have all of the ones that Mattel has released directly, and many others, including a "master set" of our buses. I have a feeling that many collectors would be jealous of my collection if I ever bothered to show it off. I have some pretty rare ones in there.

What tidbits of information about future Liberty issues can you provide for Bus collectors?
I'm very excited about the recently released Moonshine and Bootleg buses. The copper plating on the Moonshine bus turned out great, after some bit of hassle. For the Bootleg bus, we painstakingly blacked out everything, which we've never done before. Not sure if we'll ever do it again, but it looks super cool! For the future, we really hope to be more consistent with our releases – one a month is our goal. We plan to do some more variations that utilize our Liberty Legion ranks as part of the design in 2016. The higher your rank, the more limited your bus will be. We are also planning a space exploration series, which will have five buses in the series, each being released annually. Halloween will continue to be an annual tradition, while other holidays will be off and on. At some point, we'd like to start exploring some new wheels and tires, and perhaps even a whole new chassis. We'd like to offer some different options for wheels and tires from the ones that Mattel offers. I certainly would love some feedback from collectors on this.

I'd like to thank Lee for his time, and for his much-appreciated contributions to this book, and the hobby. You can see all of Liberty Promotion's upcoming offers at www.libertypromotions.com.

In this book, I've covered the two largest companies that produce the VW Bus. Is that where it ends? Absolutely not! There are some supremely talented customizers out there, and some of them have actually made a successful business out of it. As any Bus fan knows, the casting is the perfect "canvas" to work with, and there have been so many amazing issues over the years!

To me, customizing is an important part of the hobby. It allows the customizer to put themselves on the Bus, so to speak, by showing off their creative designs. It's an absolute reflection of the person creating it.

In each future volume of the *"Hot Wheels VW Bus Price Guide,"* I'll feature a talented VW Bus artist. For this volume, enter fellow North Carolinian, Bryan Pope.

I met Bryan some years ago when he attended an NCHWA show, and before he'd become the customizing guru that he is now. Pope Designs now routinely sells out each issue, and that's a direct reflection on Bryan and his dedication to putting out the absolute best product he can, each time. While his casting of choice appears to be the VW Bus, he has also customized the Dairy Delivery, Blown Delivery, Custom Convoy, '67 Camaro and other castings. The gallery that follows is a sample of his work.

Inducted into the Diecast Hall of Fame in 2010 in the "Diecast Customizers" category, Bryan continues to pursue his passion. Check him out at www.popedesigns.com.

Las Vegas 2015

Las Vegas 2015

Christmas 2014

Halloween 2014

Patriots Day 2013

Hot Wheels 45th Anniversary

Nativity Bus – Diamond Edition

Las Vegas 2013

Valentine's 2013

Christmas 2012

Nashville DCS Convention 2012

Halloween 2012

Fourth of July

Summer Smash 5 - 2012

Year of the Dragon - 2012

St. Patrick's Day

Enzo Ferrari

Wild Weekend of Hot Wheels

Hallow Bash III

Bat Pumpkin

Hot Wheels Drag Bus

Diecast HOF

Larry Wood

T1 or Not T1?

Interview With Bryan Pope of Pope Designs

What influenced you to start taking your customs to a retail level?
"After hosting a charity sale and several parties where my customs were gifts/prizes, I noticed how much in demand my customs were, and how much people personally liked them and valued them. After finally deciding to offer one of my 1 of 1 customs in a major convention auction, and it fetching $1,000, I knew I had to begin to offer my customs for sale on a wider scale."

Tough call to make, I'm sure, but which of your designs stays closest to your heart?
"Without a doubt, it would be my 2012 Christmas Nativity scene bus. That particular bus is very important to me, because it allows me to be able to express myself and my beliefs that Jesus is my Lord and savior. It was very warmly received by many of my fans and supporters."

Where do you see Pope Designs being in 5 years? Any big projects on the horizon?
"Pope Designs will be stronger than ever in five years, as I plan to utilize my upcoming 10th Anniversary to add fuel to the fire, and really bring even better customs to my fans. I don't really want to spill the beans on any future projects yet, but needless to say, people won't be disappointed!"

You've been able to travel a lot through your work. Which trip has been your favorite, so far?
"I have been fortunate to visit so many places, with so many new experience and meet so many new fans. I would have to say that, hands down, my favorite trip would be Brazil. The food, the scenery, and especially the collectors and growing customizing community were amazing! I had such a great time."

What process do you utilize to apply the deco to your models?
"I use a mixture of airbrush painting and waterslide decals. I am a graphic designer by trade, so all my graphics are original designs, created by me. I am very meticulous in applying several interwoven coats of the best quality paints I can find, along with several coats of clear coat. Then, more clear coat on top of my decals, so the finish on all my customs isn't second to anyone else's."

I'd like to thank Bryan for his time, and for sharing his work. Again, you can see Bryan's projects at www.popedesigns.com.

Production Charts

The following charts will break down the number of different VW Buses produced each year.

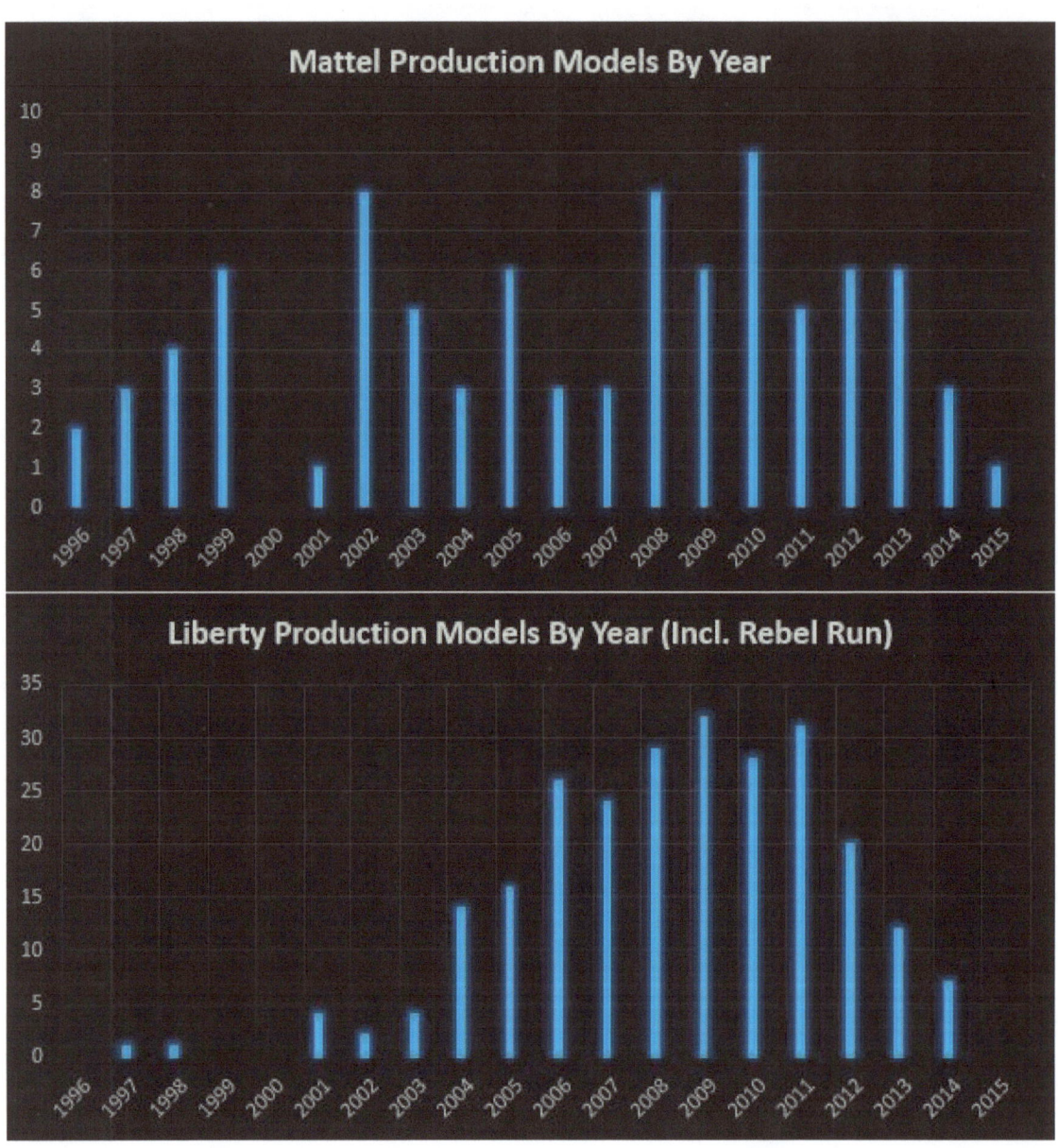

Mattel Issues

This list will give you a look at the "Top 25" most valuable Mattel VW Buses that have been issued through 2015. The list is compiled by secondary value, and not necessarily by popularity.

Rank	Year	Model	Value
1	1996	Employee Christmas (white)	2,650
2	1999	MVOA	1,500
3	2008	Redline Poker Club	710
4	2001	Penske (Burgundy)	470
5	2009	Employee Christmas (chrome)	360
6	2003	Flying Customs (Charity)	329
7	2011	Convention Finale (pink)	210
8	2010	Japan Custom Car Show (orange)	194
9	2012	Japan Convention (facing right)	190
10	2003	Hall of Fame	157
11	2012	RLC Subscription (antifreeze)	115
12	2012	Japan Convention (facing left)	115
13	2002	Phil's 10th Ann (gold, w/decal & logo)	89
14	2010	Dream Halloween	85
15	2010	Japan Custom Car Show (red)	80
16	2009	RLC (Police)	66
17	2014	RLC Gulf Racing	65
18	2002	Phil's 10th Ann (gold, w/logo, no decal)	65
19	2001	15th Convention (red flame)	64
20	2009	RLC (Fire)	62
21	2009	RLC (Taxi)	61
22	2010	Brazil Convention	60
23	2007	Osaka Convention (blue flames)	53
24	2009	RLC (Military)	53
25	2005	Treasure Hunt / Bonus	46

Liberty Promotions Issues

This list will give you a look at the "Top 25" most valuable Liberty VW Buses that have been issued through 2015. The list is compiled by secondary value, and not necessarily by popularity.

Rank	Year	Model	Value
1	2007	Pirates of the Caribbean 3 (Sneak Attack) GOLD	750
2	2007	Pirates of the Caribbean 3 (Mutineer) GOLD	680
3	2006	Pirates of the Caribbean 2 (Blackbeard) GOLD	650
4	2006	Pirates of the Caribbean 2 (Capt. Kidd) GOLD	600
5	2008	Tattoo Bus (Titanus)	397
6	2013	Brazil Wild Wing (R/Run)	151
7	2003	Kruizinwagon – Aluminum (R/Run)	150
8	2003	Kruizinwagon – Black (R/Run)	150
9	2006	Pirates of the Caribbean 2 (Capt. Kidd) SILVER	142
10	2007	Pirates of the Caribbean 3 (Mutineer) SILVER	138
11	2011	Kruizinwagon – Burnt Red (R/Run)	125
12	2006	Pirates of the Caribbean 2 (Blackbeard) SILVER	125
13	2007	Pirates of the Caribbean 3 (Sneak Attack) SILVER	122
14	2004	Dallas Convention – Sunrise	118
15	2011	Kruizinwagon – Yellow (R/Run)	118
16	2006	Bomber Bus – Yankee Gal (R/Run)	117
17	2004	Dallas Convention – Midnight Blue	113
18	2007	Surfin' Series 3 – Fire Woodie (R/Run)	108
19	2011	Summer Smash 4 – Attendee (Blue)	104
20	2007	Mexico Club (R/Run)	104
21	2012	Christmas – Mad Dasher	103
22	2006	Halloween – Vampire	102
23	2009	Winter Wagon – Snow Drift (R/Run)	102
24	2009	Superflames 2 – Burnout Bus (R/Run)	99
25	2006	Fire & Ice – Ice (R/Run)	98

There are a multitude of wheels that are used for VW Buses. Below, I've listed a few of the most common, along with the abbreviations used for them throughout the guide. (Some photo credits to Hot Wheels Wiki)

Real Riders & Standard

Accessories

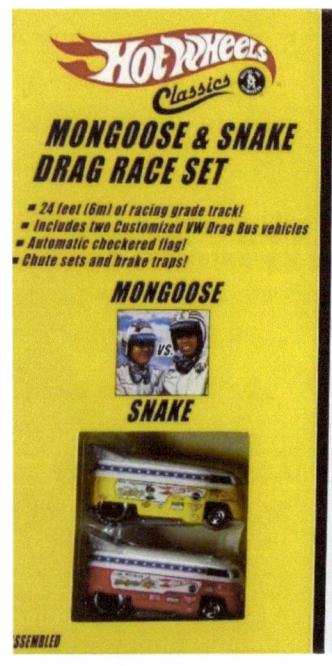

Mongoose & Snake Drag Race Set, released by HWC.com in 2005. Cover artwork is by Otto Kuhni, the very same artist who came up with the deco on the original Redline blistercards back in 1968!

Posters

Artwork has always been a major aspect of the modern diecast hobby. The blistercards that have been issued with some VW Buses have been really well-done, which adds to the collectability. As a result, that artwork has spread from the castings themselves, to a multitude of posters and E-Sheets. Here are just a few:

Spec Sheet from a 2011 K*Mart K-Days Collectors Event (Image © Mattel, Inc.)

Posters

Spec Sheet from a 2013 K*Mart K-Days Collectors Event. Notice the error, stating that it's a "T1 Drag Bus."
(Image © Mattel, Inc.)

Posters

Phil Riehlman used this poster for autographs at the 2nd Annual Hot Wheels Nationals held in Reston, Virginia in 2002. It also commemorated his 10th anniversary with Mattel. (Image © Mattel, Inc)

Posters

Autograph poster for the 2012 Super Convention in Las Vegas, Nevada. (Image © Mattel, Inc)

About The Author

Neal Giordano is a Rhode Island native who was transplanted to North Carolina in 1987, when he checked in to the Marine Corps Air Station at Cherry Point after graduating from Marine boot camp in Parris Island, South Carolina.

After serving in Operations Desert Shield and Desert Storm, he completed his Marine Corps enlistment in 1991. Today, he is currently resides in Apex, and is a Security Manager for a Fortune 500 company in Cary, North Carolina. He is also an avid Redline, Blackwall and vintage Matchbox collector.

Neal is the founder/editor of the North Carolina Hot Wheels Association website, which is one of the older Hot Wheels websites on the Internet. Through the website, he has been researching Hot Wheels values for almost 20 years. In his own words on the hobby:

"As my boys grew older, we were able to buy WAY cooler toys that piqued my interest as well. Hot Wheels were definitely something they enjoyed, and that triggered a lot of amazing memories that I had of playing with Hot Wheels and Matchbox cars as a kid."

"I missed out on the Redline era for the most part, catching only the last couple of years before the red stripes were removed from the tires. So, technically, I grew up in the Blackwall era…but, it was still a blast. We ran those cars through mud, water and who knows what else. They saw very little "track time." My parents bought me my first Hot Wheels set in 1975: the Thundershift 500. I must've logged a thousand hours on that track."

"Years later, around 1995 or so, I'm buying Hot Wheels for my boys, which got me thinking: this could be a really cool, inexpensive (don't laugh…I was completely naïve at the time!) hobby. So, I got back into Hot Wheels as an adult. Three years later, I started the North Carolina Hot Wheels Association website on Geocities, and it kept growing…and growing. It's now a massive database of Hot Wheels, from Redlines to present. It also includes vintage Lesney Matchbox guides, from the 50's through the 90's, as well as a Corgi guide."

"In the early days, the website eventually led to 7 collectors getting together in a K*Mart parking lot in Raleigh on a frigid February day in the waning days of Winter, 1998. We held a Trunk Trade, and braved the cold wind…but, everyone still enjoyed themselves. Word began to spread, and those 7 collectors eventually turned into a huge group that included collectors in Texas, South Carolina, Virginia, New Jersey and other states. We began to put on Trade Shows, where collectors could meet, buy, sell and trade. Shortly after, a few amazing members constructed an incredible downhill track, complete with 4 lanes and a digital finish line. Before we knew it, we were hosting Mattel Hot Wheels designers, and holding shows in malls that attracted collectors from all over. It was the best!"

"After a 5 year hiatus from the website, I picked up the NCHWA.com URL again in 2008, and continued what I started back in 1998."

"This publication is for all Hot Wheels collectors, young and young at heart. I'd like to personally thank all of the visitors who support NCHWA.com; you're the reason I continue to try and offer a solid resource for diecast collectors. I hope this VW Drag Bus guide helps you with your hobby."

Neal Giordano can be reached via email at nchwa@yahoo.com – email him with questions any time!
The North Carolina Hot Wheels Association website can be accessed at www.nchwa.com
You can also interact through the NCHWA Facebook page at www.facebook.com/NCHWA

Where it all began, back in 1996…Time flies!

Mattel Issues

- 15th Annual Convention (10)
- 1996 First Editions (5)
- 2002 Nationals (11)
- 30th Anniversary - boxed (6)
- 40 Years - flat-blue (18)
- All Tune & Lube (5)
- Blue Angels (7)
- Brazil Convention - 2008 (22)
- Collector Nationals -Indy (27)
- Collector's Guide CD Rom (9)
- Color Shifters - Green (28)
- Convention Finale - 2011 (24)
- Custom Car Designer (6)
- Decades - Target Excl. (12)
- Dream Halloween - 2010 (23)
- Employee Christmas - 1996 (5)
- Employee Christmas - 2009 (21)
- Flying Customs - 2002 (11)
- Flying Customs - Charity (13)
- Flying Customs - Chrome (11)
- Flying Customs - Dave Chang (13)
- Garden Grove - 2012 (25)
- Garden Grove - 2013 (27)
- Golden Knights (8)
- Gulf Racing - RLC (28)
- Hall of Fame (14)
- HW Garage - Flat Black (24)
- Internet I - Gold (6)
- Internet II - Blue (8)
- Internet III (8)
- Japan Convention - 2012 (26)
- JC Whitney (5)
- Jiffy Lube - Yellow (6)
- K-Mart Mail In - Gold (24)
- K-Mart Mail In - Pink (27)
- LA Convention - 2008 (18)
- LA Convention - 2009 (21)
- LA Convention - 2010 (22)
- LA Convention - 2011 (24)
- Light Speeders (25)
- Lucky Charms (14)
- MACE (11)
- Malleco Tower Cranes (8)
- Mexico Convention - 2008 (19)
- Mexico Convention - 2012 (25)
- Mongoose (16)
- MVOA (9)
- Mystery Car (17)
- Nationals - 2002 (11)
- Navy SEALs (7)
- Oak Brook - 2014 (28)
- Osaka Convention - 2007 (17)
- Penske - black (9)
- Penske - Burgundy (10)
- Penske - Red (10)
- Penske - Silver (9)
- Phil Riehlman - Blue (12)
- Phil Riehlman - Gold (11-12)
- Phil's Garage - B&W (22)
- Phil's Garage - Black (21)
- Phil's Garage - Blue (21)
- Phil's Garage - Orange (22)
- Pop Culture - Flash Gordon (26)
- Pop Culture - Foghorn Leghorn (28)
- Pop Culture - M&M's (29)
- Real Riders - 2004 (14)
- Real Riders - 2005 (15)
- Real Riders - 2006 (16)

Real Riders - 2007 (17)
Real Riders - 2008 (19)
Redline Poker Club (19)
RLC - 2013 (27)
RLC Fire (20)
RLC Military - (20)
RLC Neo Classics (16)
RLC Police (20)
RLC Subscription - 2012 (25)
RLC Taxi (20)
Since '68 - Green (18)
Snake (16)
Star Wars - C3PO (29)
Thank You (15)
Thunderbirds (7)
Top 40 - Yellow (18)
Treasure Hunt (15)
TRU - Aqua (13)
TRU - Orange (13)
Van de Kamps (7)
Wheaties (14)

Liberty Promotions Issues

- 9/11 Charity Bus - 2002 (30)
- Alien Bus - Abduction (38)
- Alien Bus - Autopsy (38)
- Aqua-Haulic (46)
- Bomber Bus - B17 (37)
- Bomber Bus - Happy Hour (44)
- Brazil Convention 2013 (53)
- Canada Drag Bus (46)
- Chicago Convention 2014 (54)
- Chicago Nationals - Fire (41)
- Chicago Nationals - Gangster (40)
- Chicago Nationals Charity '08 (55)
- Christmas 2012 - Mad Dasher (52)
- Christmas 2013 - Santa's Sled (53)
- Cincinnati Nationals - 48)
- Civil War - Confederate (51)
- Civil War - Union (51)
- Collection Builder - 2005 (33)
- Collector's Experience '11 Charity (60)
- Cops & Robbers - Cops (35)
- Cops & Robbers - Robbers (35)
- Dallas Convention - 2004 (31)
- Diecast HOF 2011 (48)
- Diecast HOF 2011 Charity (60)
- Diecast Super Convention (59)
- Drag-On Wagon - Green (32)
- Fighter Bus - P40 (37)
- Fire & Ice - Fire (36)
- Fire & Ice - Ice (36)
- Freaky Tiki 2 (48)
- Gear Head (45)
- Halloween 2004 (32)
- Halloween 2005 - Dungeon (34)
- Halloween 2005 - Witch (34)
- Halloween 2006 - Frankenstein (37)
- Halloween 2006 - Vampire (37)
- Halloween 2007 - Jack (39)
- Halloween 2008 - Zombie (42)
- Halloween 2009 - Werewolf (44)
- Halloween 2010 - Ghost Flames (47)
- Halloween 2011 - Gone Surfin' (50)
- Halloween 2012 - Black Widow (52)
- Halloween 2014 - Butcher (54)
- High Roller (43)
- Hot Streak - Las Vegas (51)
- HW's 40th Ann. Charity (56)
- Independence Day 2013 (53)
- Indianapolis Nationals 2013 (52)
- Kruizinwagon - Aluminum '03 (30)
- Kruizinwagon - Black '03 (31)
- Kruizinwagon - K2 Black (50)
- Kruizinwagon - K2 Red (49)
- Kruizinwagon - K2 Yellow (49)
- Lightning Wagon (42)
- Loyalty Rewards (47)
- Magical Weekend 2010 (46)
- Magical Weekend 2010 Charity (59)
- Malibu Bus (53)
- Moonshine Bus 2015 (54)
- Music City Splitty (49)
- Nationals 2009 - Reston (43)
- Nationals 2009 Charity (57)
- Outlaw Bus (44)
- Pirates 2005 - Scourge (33)
- Pirates 2005 - Treasure (33)
- Pirates 2006 - Blackbeard (36)
- Pirates 2006 - Capt. Kidd (36)
- Pirates 3 - Mutineer Bay (40)

Pirates 3 - Sneak Attack (39)
Platinum 2010 DSC (45)
RI Hot Wheels Club 2011 (50)
Route 66 (42)
Speedwagon I - (39)
Speedwagon II - (39)
St. Louis Nationals (45)
Sturgis Set 2004 - Gal (31)
Sturgis Set 2004 - Guy (32)
Sturgis Set 2005 - Gal (34)
Sturgis Set 2005 - Guy (34)
Sturgis Set 2008 (41)
Summer Smash 2008 Charity (56)
Summer Smash 2008 (41)
Summer Smash 2009 (44)
Summer Smash 2009 Charity (57)
Summer Smash 2010 (46)
Summer Smash 2010 Charity (60)
Summer Smash 2011 (49)
Summer Smash 2011 Charity (61)
Summer Smash 2012 (52)
Summer Smash 2012 Charity (61)
Super Flames I (41)
Super Flames II (42)
Super Flames III (50)
Surfin' Freaky Tiki 2 (48)
Surfin' Series 1 - Wave Rider (35)
Surfin' Series 2 - Woodie (35)
Surfin' Series 3 - Fire Woodie (38)
Surfin' Series 4 - Freaky Tiki (38)
Surfin' Series 5 - Bamboozled (40)
Surfin' Series 6 - Shark Attack (40)
Surfin' Series 7 - Cal Woodie (43)
Surfin' Series 8 - Waikiki Wagon (43)

Tattoo Bus (55)
USA Eagle Bus (47)
Van-Go! (51)
Volks-Drag'n - Pink (32)
Winter Wagon - Icicle (47)
Winter Wagon - Snow Drift (45)

Photo Credits

I'm deeply indebted to everyone who contributed pictures to this book. I couldn't have done it without you! Thanks so much!

HotWheelsCollectors.com	Pg. 14 Hall of Fame
	Pg. 23 Japan Custom Car Show (Orange)
	Pg. 27 27th Annual Convention
	Pg. 27 2013 K*Mart Mail-in
Lee Pearlman/Liberty Promotions	Entire Liberty Promotions section
Cherie Giordano	Cover Photo
	Several interior pictures
Jim Martin	Interior Cover Photo
	Several interior pictures
Brad Bannach	Several interior pictures
Bryan Pope	Entire Pope Designs section

Other Titles

HOT WHEELS TREASURE HUNT PRICE GUIDE

VOLUME 1. 1995-2014

NEAL GIORDANO

Volume I, 2015. NCHWA Publications presents a Treasure Hunt guide that spans all models from 1995-2014. Collectors will get the most current values for each model, which have all been researched with an average of 12 sample sales. The guide will assist collectors in making sound buying/selling/trading decisions, and provide interesting tidbits on the history of the Treasure Hunt segment. This guide is packed with information, to include: Current sales averages for all models, Top 25 All-Time Treasure Hunts, Top 20 All-Time Variations, Value Comparison Charts, Wheel Chart of common TH wheels, Checklists to track your collection, Treasure Hunt pictures and a complete index/car finder. An absolute power tool of information for Treasure Hunters!

Currently Available for Sale on Amazon and Barnes & Noble websites.